# The Story is Everything

## Mastering Creative Communication for Business

# Part 1: Why Storytelling Wins Every Time

CHAPTER 1  Why stories work                                8

CHAPTER 2  Feelings, actions and beliefs                   13

CHAPTER 3  Psychology, persuasion,
           presentation, story                             22

CHAPTER 4  Your audience comes first                       34

CHAPTER 5  Removing the barriers to
           communication                                   46

# Part 2: How to Build a Story

CHAPTER 6  Make structure your
           superpower                                      56

CHAPTER 7  We can all be heroes                            66

CHAPTER 8  Creativity hides in plain sight                 73

CHAPTER 9  Classic stories to have in your
           back pocket                                     80

CHAPTER 10 The elements of amazing
           storytelling                                    91

# The
# Story
# is
# Everything

**ANDREAS
LOIZOU**

To Helena, with love and gratitude

First published in Great Britain in 2022 by
Laurence King Student & Professional
An imprint of Quercus Editions Ltd
Carmelite House
50 Victoria Embankment
London EC4Y 0DZ

An Hachette UK company

A CIP catalogue record for this book is available from the British
Library

PB ISBN 978-1-91394-794-1
Ebook ISBN 978-1-52941-973-3

10 9 8 7 6 5 4 3 2 1

Design by TwoSheds

Printed and bound in China by C&C Offset Printing Co., Ltd.

Papers used by Laurence King Publishing are from well-managed
forests and other responsible sources.

## Part 3: How to Be a Fantastic Storyteller

CHAPTER 11  Finding your storytelling voice  104

CHAPTER 12  What is flow, and why does it feel so damn good?  112

CHAPTER 13  Creating your ideal conditions  120

CHAPTER 14  Ways to improve your writing style  128

CHAPTER 15  Polish that diamond  136

## Part 4: What We Learn from the Masters

CHAPTER 16  Ethos, pathos and logos  146

CHAPTER 17  Reading for fun and for profit  155

CHAPTER 18  Turning dull data into exciting stories  165

CHAPTER 19  Grab 'em with headlines and loglines  175

CHAPTER 20  Where to now?  184

Index  190

Acknowledgements  192

# PART 1

# Why Storyt Wins E Time

# elling
# very

# CHAPTER 1

# Why stories work

Stories change people. Since our cave-dwelling days we've enjoyed sitting around the fire to talk and to listen. Our brains are magically transformed by stories, creating fresh pathways where new tales wipe out old ways of thinking and acting.

# Like me, you prefer short intros

## We love great stories even more than we hate terrible presentations.

We are all natural-born storytellers. Our listeners admire our honesty when we admit our mistakes, and they cheer as we conquer the obstacles in our path. They identify with us even as we excite and inspire them. Our success – as wizened CEO or fresh-faced whizz-kid – is their success.

Storytelling creates an emotional connection that mere facts can never attain. You won't make a connection with your ninety-nine bullets about sales targets and employee churn rate. Reciting dull data isn't enough. That guy in row three may look as though he's listening, but real influence comes only when you change what's in his heart.

We all want our tales to be so exciting, instructive or funny that people repeat them. You've made a great choice, because this book will show you how.

# How I wrote this chapter

## Introductions are hard to write. You're never sure if they will be read – like prefaces and acknowledgements, they're generally skipped by readers who are hungry for the good stuff.

So, I decided to start with Chapter 1 instead. Novels don't have introductions, and I'm always advising my clients to jump right into their tale. There's no point dilly-dallying when there's a story to be shared.

At this stage you'll have liked the name of the book, its cover and its general design, size and feel. It follows that anyone reading this sentence in a bookshop or on Amazon is close to being a buyer. Don't muck it up, I'm telling myself, make sure this first chapter is a winner.

The opening chapter sets the tone for the whole book. So I've made sure that it reflects the content and structure of *The Story Is Everything*.

→ **I start off with why stories win over audiences.**

When I picture you, I see someone who is smart and eager
to learn, yet slightly sceptical. You'll be pushed for time, so
there's no point in writing 800 pages on literary theory. But
you may also be frustrated by the books you've read recently
on business storytelling, which pad out a single idea with
examples you've seen before. I'm fed up of buying books that
have barely enough content for a single chapter. I want my
readers to know that there are lots of reasons why stories win.

→ **Then I show you how to build a story.**

I love structure, especially when it's hidden. Did you find mine
in the opening section? I know you'll skim the first words of
each paragraph while you're deciding to buy, so I deliberately
front-loaded each sentence with my most important points:

**We love stories**
**Stories change people**
**We are all natural-born storytellers**
**Storytelling creates an emotional connection**
**We all want our tales to be exciting, instructive or funny**

I decided against putting a personal story in Chapter 1.
Competing books tend to have a tale about a massive
personal breakthrough, a moment of epiphany when the
author realizes her slides aren't making an impression or
a big contract is lost because she can't connect with the
audience. I will show you the impact of storytelling on my
life, but I'll reveal it slowly.

By the time you've finished this book, you'll be peppering
your conversation with 'hero's journey', 'narrative arc' and
'plot points'. But it'll take time and work to make this happen.
The book demands input from you: commit to the exercises,
read with a pen in your hand, write your ideas down. Creation
is an active process, so be prepared to roll up your sleeves and
get messy.

→ **Next I'll share loads of ideas on how to become a fantastic storyteller.**

Voice is key. Throughout *The Story Is Everything* I use the pronoun 'we' to suggest that my readers and I want the same benefits when we communicate. We're in this together; it's only us who can save the world from dull PDF handouts.

But I also 'talk' to *you* directly, as if we were in a conversation. This sense of dialogue is important to me. I'm a friendly adviser, not an aloof lecturer. The occasional rhetorical question increases this sense of face-to-face communication. That's an effective technique, isn't it?

I want to come across as someone with useful ideas, but not a show-off. I'll present both sides of an argument because I rarely have an axe to grind. But I avoid the language of doubt ('I hope to', 'this might possibly work'), because you want to trust me as an authority.

→ **We'll finish off with what we can learn from the masters of communication.**

My dominant tone is positivity. Psychologists have taught me to emphasize your gains ('You will benefit in many ways by improving your storytelling skills') rather than your losses ('Don't be dumb and miss out on learning this topic').

| Why Storytelling Wins Every Time | How to Build a Story |
|---|---|
| Your audience<br>Feelings, actions, beliefs<br>Influence | Your creativity<br>Structures<br>Heroes and villains |
| **THE STORY IS EVERYTHING** | |
| How to Be a Fantastic Storyteller | What We Learn from the Masters |
| Your voice<br>Flow<br>Editing | Your impact<br>Facts into stories<br>Grabbing their attention |

Experts on influence and persuasion have warned me away from being too strident. If I spend the whole chapter banging on about how fantastic the book is, you will end up feeling manipulated. 'Always be closing' may be a great mantra for the salesmen in *Glengarry Glen Ross*, but it's the wrong approach for a book that you are choosing to buy and read.

I'm convinced that writing success comes from planning. I wrote this opening chapter only once I'd finished the rest of the book. Believe me, knowing how your story ends is a huge help at the beginning.

## Where to Next?

→ You can read *The Story Is Everything* in chapter order, but the book is also designed for you to jump to topics that currently spark your interest. I'll list possible next steps at the end of every chapter, except for this one. Now I want you to do the logical thing and go straight to Chapter 2. After that, you're free to roam.

# Feelings, actions and beliefs

Business storytelling is about influence. You know a story works when it changes the feelings, actions or thoughts of your audience.

# A great storyteller knows how to influence

An influential storyteller changes people. Their tales excite you or make you anxious. They can make you reject capitalism, change your mind about recycling or spend £200 on a pair of trainers that cost £2 to make.

Let's look at feelings, actions and beliefs in more detail.

### → Feelings

These are the instinctive reactions we experience when we see a smiling child or a starving animal, when we learn that our team has won the cup or that someone we love has died. Although most of us use 'feelings' and 'emotions' as interchangeable words, there's a subtle (yet very important) difference: think of feelings as the physical and mental representation of an emotion.

### → Actions

We may want our listeners to change their behaviour or act in a certain way. It could be simple ('Buy this great book you are currently flicking through') or more nuanced ('Keep yourself isolated to avoid infecting others'). Slogans that begin with an imperative verb want the reader to do something – Interflora has been telling us to 'Say it with flowers' since 1917.

For every Happy and Glorious Occasion

*Say it with Flowers*

What nicer way of conveying greetings than by a gift of beautiful flowers? Within a matter of hours, fresh, untravelled flowers can be delivered anywhere in Gt. Britain, the Commonwealth and other countries of the free world through members of Interflora.

**INTERFLORA**
The International FLOWERS-BY-WIRE SERVICE

Order only through florists displaying the above symbol—your guarantee of satisfaction.

Issued by INTERFLORA (Dept. Q) 358/362 KENSINGTON HIGH ST., W.14

Interflora's slogan has been successful for more than 100 years.

### → <u>Beliefs</u>

Our thoughts reflect the way we perceive and interpret the world. Our experiences mould the way we think, especially when we're young; for example, I have always thought that dogs are dangerous because I saw one bite my dad when I was 7 years old. Our thoughts are also formed by evidence, facts, the opinions of our peers, social-media influencers and a host of other sources. We *believe* our beliefs have a rational basis. That's not always the case.

A word of caution. Our real-life use of these and similar words is imprecise. One person may use 'gut feeling' to describe their thoughts, another may regard the phrase 'belief system' as synonymous with 'intellectual ideas'. Don't worry; as long as the distinction between the emotional and intellectual responses is clear, you'll be OK.

| Feel | Act | Believe |

Feelings, actions and beliefs give us the handy acronym **FAB**. I'm not a big fan of acronyms, especially in the business world, but I'll mention FAB frequently during *The Story Is Everything*.

# The perfect pitch?

**Every emotional person has rational thoughts; every rational thinker has emotions.**

Sometimes the same communication can simultaneously target feelings, actions and beliefs. A great story causes a change in beliefs and thoughts, and this often leads to a change in the way people act. Let's take a look at the health technology corporation Theranos and its charismatic boss, Elizabeth Holmes, a woman who often crossed the line between inspired CEO and crazed cult leader.

## → An appeal to the emotions

Holmes famously talked about her uncle during TED talks and investor pitches. His death had galvanized her to drop out of Stanford University and develop blood-testing machines that would give faster results:

> I remember his love of crossword puzzles and trying to teach us to play football. I remember how much he loved the beach. I remember how much I loved him.
>    He was diagnosed one day with skin cancer, which all of a sudden was brain cancer and in his bones. He didn't live to see his son grow up, and I never got to say goodbye.

Holmes's appeal to our emotions creates many responses. We empathize with her sense of loss because we've all had friends and family who've died before their time. Instead of a polished entrepreneur pitching for equity investors, we see the little girl skipping across the sands. Our brains make an imaginative leap: we now understand that her motivation is to save lives, not to become rich. The speed of the uncle's illness – 'one day', 'all of a sudden' – contrasts with the slow pace of his idyllic life with its beach, crossword puzzles and time to play. The message is that better testing might have detected his illness earlier and given him a chance to see his son grow up.

## → An appeal to the rational thinker

But Holmes was also adept at appealing to the rational part of an investor's brain. Her pitches referred to successful trials of Edison, the company's testing machine, which could miraculously analyse a single drop of blood and produce a battery of results in minutes. Reams of printouts were produced as evidence. Scientists held up graphs that displayed Edison's effectiveness.

Elizabeth Holmes became the world's youngest self-made billionaire.

Holmes's double-pronged approach – emotional storytelling *and* scientific backup – opened the minds and wallets of investors. She got her desired action: at the age of 30 Elizabeth Holmes became the world's youngest self-made billionaire and one of the richest women on the planet. A shame, then, that she wasn't very close to the uncle and all the evidence about Edison had been faked.

To find out more about what happened at Theranos you must read John Carreyrou's *Bad Blood: Secrets and Lies in a Silicon Valley Startup* (2018), but to be honest the subtitle gives you a pretty big clue. If you want to see Holmes in action, it's worth checking out the HBO documentary *The Inventor: Out for Blood in Silicon Valley* (2019), directed by Alex Gibney.

# How influencers create stories in our minds

We've all got a John Bowes in our office. That quiet guy, does something with computers, smiles at you in the lift, but you've never had a chat with him. To be honest, you're not really sure who John is or what he does.

Which is quite a problem, because HR have told you to organize John's leaving party. You sent an email to all 400 people in the firm on Monday, but so far you've had zero replies. Now it's Friday afternoon and you need a new approach. Or – to be more accurate – approaches.

How can you use Feelings, Actions and Beliefs to create a new message that will get more people to John's party? Here are some suggestions that have worked in the past for people who are significantly less popular than you or me.

## → Appeal to BELIEF.

Get people to think differently about John.

You tell people what John has done for them: 'John, who's been processing all your expense claims these last four years ...'

You position John as someone who might help them in the future. He's no longer the office nerd, but a person of influence: 'John's leaving us to be head of customer experience at our much bigger competitor ...'

## → Call to ACTION.

Get people to do something for John (or themselves).

You change the perception of the evening, from John's goodbye party to a chance to grab something for nothing. Whether John notices that people are there for him or the drink is another matter: 'Come to the pub early. There's a free drink for anyone who's there before 6pm ...'

You accept that, to be brutally honest, John's not that important. So, you hijack his night and turn it into a Departmental Event: 'It's been ages since we've all been out together, so let's make John's party a special night for all of us ...'

## → Connect on an EMOTIONAL level.

Get people to feel something about John.

You say more about what John does, but this time frame it in a more emotional context. He's dedicated his working life to making sure we get paid on time, so the least we can do is stand him a drink: 'John's worked so hard to speed up repayments of our expenses, and it will be a great shame for us to lose his expertise ...'

You can even stray into Elizabeth Holmes territory, and cross the line between influence and manipulation: 'Imagine how you would feel if no one said goodbye when you left ...'

# FAB in finance

**Do you believe that we're rational beings when it comes to the dollars and yen in our pocket? Think again. Behavioural finance is the study of how our emotions affect our financial decisions.**

Financial services are difficult to advertise. They're invisible and, to be frank, rather boring. Just whisper the phrase 'financial planning' to a friend and watch their eyelids droop and close. We know money is important, but most of us would rather eat glass than phone a call centre. We might be furious with an overdraft charge or smash our phone on the table when we're put on hold for the ninth time, but the vast majority of us are completely inert when it comes to changing bank. And one bank seems very similar to another, so why bother?

Advertisers need to get their message across quickly. In the three ads shown overleaf, you'll see how targeting Feelings, Actions and Beliefs helps them to connect to the part of you that responds. In ten words or fewer their slogans create *micro-stories* in our minds.[1]

The Lloyds advert is an appeal to the emotions. The phrase 'family matters' has at least two meanings; it signifies 'family is important' and also hints at that fat Manila envelope, hidden in a drawer that we can never prise open, where we keep cancelled passports, old insurance documents and that draft of our last will and testament. The girl seems to be happily taking her first steps towards independence, but the top half of the guiding, supporting adult by her side is missing. There's an uneasy sense of loss in this picture, a threat to the simple joys of a summer's day. It's time for you, as a responsible adult, to take control of the paperwork and plan for the future.

---

1    You'll find more about micro-stories in Chapter 3.

**Top:** Lloyds taps in to our deep emotions ...
**Above, left:** ... while Ally plays on our laziness ...
**Above, right:** ... and ING focuses on the facts.

The Ally ad is a play on customer inertia. It offers a way to open a new savings account without having to move away from your current bank. Ally is online only and markets mostly to millennials in the US; its customers are tech-savvy and very happy *not* to have to speak to bank staff. It's an appeal to action ('switch') that demands minimal effort.

ING is colder and more rational in its approach. There is no place for emotions or relationships in this bank. Instead, it attracts customers with facts and evidence. There's no fee, and in an expensive world that's a very compelling message.

Banks realized many years ago that while some people are motivated by percentage points and branch opening hours, many others are dependent on emotions – fear, greed, gratification, joy – of which they may not even be aware. Marketing departments know that the most sensitive nerve in a human's body leads from the heart to the bank account. Stories, images and slogans all help them to target our Feelings, Actions and Beliefs.

## Where to Next?

→ To follow up these themes, look at:

- Chapter 3: Four simple structures for micro-stories.
- Chapter 10: Tips on creating pictures in a reader's mind.
- Chapter 18: How to grip your audience with graphs and evidence.

→ Think about this. Become super-aware of adverts. The advertisers have milliseconds to grab you. What element of FAB (Feelings, Actions and Beliefs) do they focus on? Pay particular attention to the first word you see. I'm in my local coffee bar and just ten seconds on Facebook gives me 'Swap', 'Leave', 'Join', 'Save', 'Enjoy', 'Visit' and 'Share'. A glance at my fellow coffee-drinkers proves the impact of 'Just Do It', 'Think Different' and 'Have a Break, Have a KitKat'.

# CHAPTER 3

# Psychology, persuasion, presentation, story

Humans all over the world are susceptible to the same influences. You can add these triggers to even the simplest stories to create emotional resonance.

# We are all influenced by stories

**No one knows more about influencing people than the social psychologist Robert Cialdini. He spent many years undercover at used-car showrooms and call centres learning how advertisers and marketers change our minds.**

Cialdini's analysis of charity fundraisers, cold-callers and waitresses eager for bigger tips reveals the triggers that open our wallets and purses. His most illuminating research was carried out in the 1970s and 1980s, well before the arrival of the internet. But his findings are more applicable now than ever. Technology hasn't changed fundamental human behaviours, but it has speeded them up.

Cialdini heard stories every day. He learned that our behaviour is governed by entirely predictable forces. Short stories – even specific words – can turn a cautious browser into a hot prospect.

Cialdini's *Influence: The Psychology of Persuasion* (1984) has had a big impact on me ever since I found three copies of the book in my tutor's study overlooking Christ's Pieces in Cambridge. This wasn't absent-mindedness on her part; she wanted to convince her students of how Cialdini's principles explain six universal facets of human behaviour. I've still got my half-page summary:

1. Reciprocity – we return favours
2. Commitment and consistency – we tend to stick to our beliefs
3. Social proof – we copy others, so often find it hard to go against groupthink
4. Liking – we like people who share our goals and who are similar to us
5. Authority – we listen to experts (and people who pretend to be experts, as well)
6. Scarcity – we don't like being left out

# How I use influence in my storytelling

**I'm not a person who's hampered by crippling self-doubt, so please forgive me for drawing examples from an article I wrote for _The Bookseller_ in 2018 about the Margate Bookie, the charity I set up to bring people together through reading and writing.**

I didn't write the article with Cialdini in mind. Instead, the ideas came to me on a long walk along the beach. I recorded my thoughts as my feet crunched over the gritty sand and got splashed in rock pools, wrote them up in an hour at home and had an article ready by the end of the evening. I sent it to a couple of friends for feedback, but it came out of my mind naturally, without force or manipulation. Without realizing it, I'd used five of Cialdini's principles in an article of less than one thousand words. We use them all the time, even when we're not conscious of them.

Make your stories as personal as possible.

→ **We trust people who are authorities.**

People are more likely to read an article about setting up a literary festival if it's written by someone who's actually done it. We all listen to the person with the battle scars and the war stories, and ignore the report-writer with his dry-as-dust *How to Effectively Programme Manage a Book Festival*, complete with impenetrable 9-metre flow chart.

And we respect people who've been transformed by difficult situations. My first sentence draws people in with its hints of emotional and financial pain. The last two sentences show that I've learned and grown: 'When you regenerate a town, you regenerate its people. And that includes me.'

## → Consistency and commitment make people stick with you.

I wanted to show that I was a man of my word. If I was going to start a festival, I was damn well going to make sure it was a success. Going public with my plans was a commitment to the town.

I'm happy with the growth of the festival, but more important for me are connecting with new people and feeling part of a community. To be consistent, the wonderful team behind the Bookie works hard to keep these ideals at the centre of the festival.

## → We like people who are similar to us.

It sounds obvious, but our friends tend to have similar tastes and interests to us. This common ground unites us, gives us fresh things to talk about and encourages us to share. The article stresses that the festival is enjoyable for audience and writers ('they came because it was fun'), which removes the fear that it's going to be stuffy and formal. Calling the town 'small, friendly and cheerful' and saying 'I decided to throw a party' tells readers that it was an event where they would meet like-minded souls.

## → People like to return favours.

Cialdini's Principle of Reciprocity states that doing good unto others is the best way for others to do good unto you. This is a long way from consciously scratching the backs of people more important than you. It's about treating authors with respect, looking after our volunteers and making sure our audience has a great time.

→ **Social proof keeps our audience growing.**

The hardest part of any new venture is finding your first supporters. Once you've got them, others follow. I name-dropped some famous authors into the story, because I wanted people to know that I had the clout and contacts to attract star authors to our town. There's a power in association. Famous authors sell more tickets, but they also show other authors that Margate is worth a visit. And because our authors come from different backgrounds, our audience gets more diverse.

Our main venue – the world-famous Turner Contemporary gallery – also gives us high social worth. If the festival is good enough to be held there, then it must be worth visiting.

# What the Spanish Christmas lottery tells us about storytelling and influence

**The motivation for buying a lottery ticket is normally clear. Either you want to join the ranks of the super-rich, or you believe in supporting the charities that benefit from a slice of the profits.**

But *el Gordo* (literally 'the fat one') has a different remit. At €200, the tickets are pricy, which forces people to club together to buy them. Most people buy a *décimo*, one tenth of a ticket. The top prize is €4 million, which means the most they can win is €400,000. That's not to be sniffed at, of course, but it's a long way shy of the world's largest individual payout on the Mega Millions lottery of $1.537 billion. Yes, billion.

Why do the Spanish participate with such enthusiasm? The lottery's strapline gives a big clue: 'the greatest prize is sharing'. *Décimos* – and their smaller relatives *participaciónes* – are available at your gym, the local butcher and your hairdressing salon. Friends and colleagues form syndicates and promise to share any prizes. 'What will you do with your slice of the jackpot?' is a half-serious, half-joky question you'll hear before the big draw on 22 December.

The advertising agency Contrapunto BBDO was charged with repositioning the tickets as a holiday gift. They produced micro-dramas, each no longer than 90 seconds, that use the principle of influence to change a buyer's FAB. Spain is a country where the bond between family members is highly valued, and the adverts focus on the emotional connection between two people in an awkward family scenario. The three movies are masterpieces of influence:

### → The new boyfriend

A father has three daughters. The youngest brings her new, nervous boyfriend to Christmas dinner. The dad, who's not keen at all, has bought *décimos* for everyone except the new kid. But when the potential son-in-law lets slip that he's bought them tickets, the dad frantically adds the boy's name to an envelope ...

It's reciprocity in action. The boy gives something to the dad, the dad feels obliged to give something to the boy in return. And, with that tiny exchange of gifts, a new member is welcomed into the family in time for Christmas.

### → *Succession* in miniature

A daughter has been chosen to run her father's factory, but he can't quite say goodbye to all he has created. She hands her reluctant dad a ticket. The numbers she picked are the date that he opened his factory forty years ago.

The daughter symbolically assumes her inheritance. She shows that she is similar to her father in values, sentiment and ambition. She knows how much the business means to him, and she won't let him down.

### → The estranged daughter-in-law

A father-in-law visits his ex-daughter-in-law. He's not a man used to sharing his emotions, but he reduces her (and us) to tears when he hands her a ticket – 'because even though you're no

The new boyfriend faces his potential in-laws for the first time.

longer my son's wife, to me you'll always be part of the family'.

Consistency tells us that, even if situations and relationships change, the people who are important will always be close to us.

This Christmas I'm going to buy a couple of *participaciónes*, maybe even a *décimo*, at Aroma y Bread, my local coffee shop. These three stories have stuck with me in a way that a thousand people shouting 'The lottery brings people together' would never do.

# Micro-stories influence your listener

**Micro-stories are those short tales we share, almost in passing, with one or two other people. They are the 'urban myths' of a company that you hear all the time if you're working at a big organization.**

These stories don't need a huge budget or Hollywood-scale production values. There's just enough detail for the listener to connect with your worldview, but not enough to get in the way of the message.

I'll give you examples of four types of micro-story, set in the past, the present, the immediate future and the far future. After each example I want you to write down your idea. This isn't a test of your writing skills. What I want is for you to use your memory and your imagination to come up

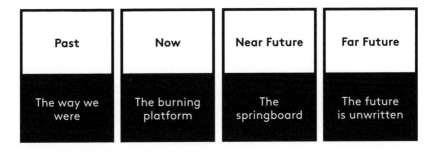

with the example at the centre of each idea. If you write full sentences, that's great, but don't feel obliged to.

### → In the past: The way we were

This isn't a nostalgic plea for a golden era that never existed, but a way to highlight what's changed. Sometimes it's about what you've lost: 'We used to spend more time getting to know each of our customers before we focused on costs.' Or it could be about what you've gained: 'Our customers love the fact that they can now order direct from the warehouse without having to speak to sales and accounts.'

*The Way We Were* stories are easy to write; you just need to make clear what's changed between the past and the present day. These stories are more effective when you let listeners come to their own conclusions about whether the change is positive or negative, rather than ramming a moral down their throats.

For example, the fashion industry is rife with greenwashing, where companies run misleading marketing campaigns and pay celebrities to endorse their bogus environmental policies. Before Covid-19, many customers accepted these claims at face value. Now consumers do more research to identify dishonest brands.

*What did we do in the past?*
*How do we do it differently now?*

### → In the present: The burning platform

Fear is a great motivator. Burning platform stories stress that change is needed right now, not in the future. No one waits for instructions from a steering committee when their floor is on fire.

Every other book on business storytelling has a chapter about Apple. But it's much more instructive, and far more original, to look at businesses that were destroyed by Apple. The Finnish tech giant Nokia was once the world leader in mobile phones. But it focused on hardware rather than software, and believed its brand was strong enough to see off the competition. After all, it had been the first company to create a cellular network.

The problem was that data, rather than voice, began to drive demand for mobile phones. Nokia didn't respond to the changing demands of its users, so its market share collapsed. In 2013 Microsoft bought Nokia's smartphone business for $7.6 billion, only to write off its investment as worthless less than two years later. Sadly, 7,800 jobs were lost. Nokia's failure to predict the importance of software, and its unwarranted belief in the value of its brand, caused the company's collapse.

Critics complain that burning platform stories are inherently negative because they point out a problem without suggesting a solution. But that's not their *raison d'être*. They're a shock, not an answer. Burning platform stories spread whenever a complacent company is threatened by a disruptive new entrant. They describe the moment a fax machine manufacturer received its first order via email, or the first evening the CEO of Blockbuster stayed in to watch Netflix.

Your burning platform story only needs two elements. Give it a go!

*What's the problem?*
*What happens if I do nothing about it?*

### → In the near future: The springboard

Springboard stories are always positive. Beginning in the near past, they describe how a single individual benefited from conquering a challenge. It's the learner driver who passed on his twentieth attempt, the drifting teenager who found her purpose in life after appearing at her first poetry slam.

A successful springboard story acts as an example for the future of the whole organization. If he can stick at the driving, or if she can face down her stage fright, then I can too. Because springboard stories start in the past, listeners instinctively trust them to be true. The positive outcome inspires them to act. 'Parable' is probably too loaded a word, but you get the idea.

Jack Ma is the richest man in China, worth a staggering $25 billion at the time of writing. His e-commerce giant, Alibaba, sells more than eBay and Amazon together. (Stop for a second and think just how many parcels that looks like.) But Ma was, by his own admission, a terrible student who continually failed his exams. He was shunned by every employer he approached. He tells the story of how he was the only person to be rejected by the interviewers at KFC.

Ma failed in the traditional routes of Chinese society. But he succeeded when he realized he was a natural entrepreneur. His most famous quotation reads like a springboard story:

*Never give up. Today is hard, tomorrow will be worse, but the day after tomorrow will be sunshine.*

Springboard stories can also be reduced to two elements:

**What was I failing at?**
**How did it feel when I succeeded?**

### → In the far future: The future is unwritten

My scepticism alarm beeps loudly when I hear phrases like 'roadmap to excellence' and 'blue-sky thinking'. It's hard to convince people about a future that's far away; we can't visualize the speaker's dreams and we've all been let down by corporate evangelists. Too enthusiastic and we distrust the speaker; too matter-of-fact and we respond with a collective yawn.

Successful ads combine emotional appeal with hard evidence.

This anti-smoking ad from Australia is a clever twist on The Future Is Unwritten. It appears to focus on evidence. Stop smoking and the statistics of your life will change – you will *gain* 30 per cent, *save* $4,000 and *halve* risks. But the ad's emotional appeal is all about what the future will bring you. Your sense of taste and smell will get better, your skin may improve, your heart and lungs will be healthier. But the real beneficiary will be the child you've probably not even thought about yet -- stop smoking before getting pregnant and your risk of having a pre-term baby is the same as for a non-smoker.

It takes a genius to make stories set in the far future seem credible. Handle them with care unless you have Nelson Mandela-level rhetorical skills. Again, you need two elements to make this work:

1.  Describe your vision with clarity. Tell the audience what it looks like. You have to spend time giving details.
2.  Describe the impact of your vision with emotion. This isn't the place for statistics and dry forecasts; instead, tell your listeners what emotions they will feel when your vision comes to life for them.

*What's your vision?*
*What will be the emotional impact of your vision on the audience?*

# Where to Next?

→ **To follow up these themes, look at:**

- **Chapter 12:** If you found the exercises too difficult, consider flow. You'll find flow when the degree of challenge matches your ability.

- **Chapter 17:** One of the best ways to learn how to write is to read the work of authors you love.

→ **Watch more adverts!** What Cialdini principles do the most effective ones employ?

# CHAPTER 4

# Your audience comes first

Focus on your readers and listeners at all times. Writing with an audience in mind automatically improves your readability and choice of words.

# Thank you for buying my book

**How did you decide to buy it? Maybe you picked it off the bestsellers' table at the front of a shop, attracted by the cover or the title.**

Perhaps you flicked from the front to the back, looking for the structure and the book's narrative flow, or maybe you held it up as if you were weighing it. Did it strike you as a heavy or light book?

Perhaps you found it on Amazon, marvelling at the pictures and graphics as you skimmed through a sample. Were you swayed or irritated by the online reviewers? Did the big quotations scattered through the book pull you in? Was price a factor?

Everybody judges *before* reading a book or listening to a story. People make their decision in seconds. Three decades of internet browsing have given us the attention span of a small, not particularly smart chicken. We're ruthless.

The first step in business writing isn't coming up with a dramatic opening, a brand tie-in or a dramatic retelling of that time you sold your first event ticket. No, it's thinking long and hard about your audience and what they want from you. You might be the best storyteller in the world, but if your audience isn't interested in your tale, you're selling double glazing to someone who doesn't have any windows.

# You need to show your audience a reason to listen

**There are three reasons readers or an audience will give you their valuable time.**

→ **Your story is useful.** What you're telling them will benefit them right now. By the time you've finished your piece, they will have something they can use immediately.

→ **Your story is interesting.** They'll learn something from you that will help them in the future. Your ideas about parenting or retirement homes aren't needed right now, but ten, twenty years later they'll remember your talk. And hopefully your name.

→ **Your story is enjoyable.** It makes them laugh, moves them to tears, makes them remember what it was like to be ambitious or inspired. On a mundane day in a beige world, you stood out by being exciting and original.

My examples come from a battered guidebook I found in a hippie café in Kathmandu. I was planning to trek the Annapurna trail but, to be honest, a lazy fortnight on a beach was more appealing. In the end this second-hand book, which I bought for the equivalent of half a euro, got me going.

> Useful: what buses to take from downtown Kathmandu to the start of the trail
>
> Interesting: the ten essential sights on the trail (I saw six of them)
>
> Enjoyable: a brief history of Nepal and an introduction to local customs and even the language. *Namaskara!*

Your story should land somewhere in the triangle of useful, interesting and enjoyable. It's better to be really strong in one area than just about appear in two. It's impossible to be strong in all three areas simultaneously unless you are an absolute master! If you don't feature in any of the three areas, save your breath and rethink. What can you change about your story to make it more appealing?

The best 50 cents I ever spent.

# Top tips to keep your audience with you for the entire journey

### → Begin with the ending in mind.

Every word in your story must move you purposefully closer to the ending. You must know the *what* of the ending (e.g. the executive coach had faked her formal qualifications in psychology) and also the *why* (e.g. we often rush due diligence of plausible people).

A flat ending often follows a meandering middle. Influence is impossible if you're not clear about the change you want to happen. You're the designated driver in the room. People are relying on you to know the final destination before you set out.

### → Open strongly.

You're probably not going to come up with a first line of the calibre of 'The past is a foreign country; they do things differently there,' or 'It was a queer, sultry summer, the summer they electrocuted the Rosenbergs, and I didn't know what I was doing in New York.'[1] But you do need to show, at a minimum, that you are delivering a story rather than a run-of-the-mill presentation.

You can start by introducing the hero or villain. Use variants along the lines of 'Here's Jennifer, who graduated with a big problem,' or 'Meet Geoffrey, who ordered more bananas than any other client in 2021.' Anchoring your tale firmly in the past sends the audience a signal that a story is about to begin. People's expectations change when they hear phrases such as 'I first saw Ellam talking at the Poetry Slam' or 'I spent my first two years as a doctor hiding my fear of blood.'

### → Practice lets you improvise.

I rehearse a lot – and I mean a lot – before I tell a story in public. I want to come across as relaxed and in control of the room, but to do that well I have to know my story inside out. With

---

1    L.P. Hartley, *The Go-Between* (1953); Sylvia Plath, *The Bell Jar* (1963).

a strong foundation, I feel comfortable adding new lines or strolling around the room. I use a voice recorder to fix my version of the story in my memory, and I often present to a video camera to check that my body language matches my words.

Thinking of using notes because you're nervous? Don't. And don't rely on your PowerPoint slides as a crutch, either. It's better to work on your confidence than to show people you haven't bothered to learn your lines. If you have prepared sufficiently, the story will come to you as easily as leaves appear on a tree in springtime.

## If content is king, simplicity is queen

**No amount of style can redeem poor content. But poor style can destroy fantastic content. Achieving a style that is clear, precise and easy to understand is not an option but a necessity.**

We consider factors such as voice and writing style later on in 'How to Be a Fantastic Storyteller' (Part 3), but for now let's focus on readability. Although this is primarily about written text, my methods to improve readability are directly applicable to spoken presentations as well.

→ **The two components of readability are sentence length and word choice.**

No one wants to reread a sentence. The first time it happens, readers blame themselves for not paying attention. The second time, they'll feel uneasy about their abilities. The third time, they'll blame the writer. If your work is unclear, imprecise, vague or difficult, readers have plenty of alternatives. We're all busy, and writers who waste the reader's time won't get followers.

→ **The Flesch Reading Ease score is the most common measure of readability for English-language texts.**

It rewards short words and tight sentences with a high score, and penalizes multi-syllabic words and lengthy sentences with a low score.

The Flesch score was devised for use in English but has been adapted, with varying degrees of success, for other languages. The score must be adjusted when you're looking at another language, but the principle – short words in short sentences – stays exactly the same.

| Flesch Reading Score | |
| --- | --- |
| 90 | **Very Easy**<br>Understood by an average 11-year-old |
| 65 | **'Plain English'**<br>Easily understood by a 14-year-old |
| 40 | **Difficult**<br>Pitched at the level of first year in tertiary education |
| 20 | **Very difficult**<br>You need a degree to understand this |
| 5 | **Extremely difficult**<br>You need to be an expert in the field |

The higher the score, the easier the text is to read.

A score of 100 means that pretty much every adult will understand you; a score of 0 means it's *Finnegans Wake* by James Joyce. Or this, from the disgraced ex-CEO of McDonalds, Steve Easterbrook:

*In conjunction with our refranchising plans, we will take a market-by-market approach, set higher financial screens for markets operating company-operated restaurants, and leverage both conventional and developmental licensee structures across the segments.*

Business writing is full of rubbish like this. I needed six or seven attempts to work out what I think he means, and even now I'm not entirely sure. My perception of the writer worsened with each read-through. I'm left with the belief that there are three reasons Easterbrook can't explain his strategy:

1. He's a poor communicator
2. He doesn't consider his audience to be important
3. He fundamentally doesn't understand the topic

# You are responsible for improving readability

**No one will ever ask you to make your writing more complicated.**

Never blame your audience for failing to understand your writing. If your writing is impenetrable, there are many ways to make it easier to understand.

→ <u>Limit yourself to one idea per sentence.</u>

This will stop the piling up of embedded clauses, those half-sentences nestling within other half-sentences, that should be either deleted or turned into sentences of their own.

The statistics analysing the relationship between sentence length and lost readers are terrifying.[2] If your average sentence length is 25 words, you risk losing a third of your readership, *even if they are interested in your topic.* Easterbrook's sentence quoted above (one of the shortest in a longer statement) comes in at 35 words. Reading a full page of that is like deciphering a lost language.

---

2    The statistics that follow refer to writing in English. They'll be different for other languages.

| Word count | Reader comprehension | Readers lost |
|------------|---------------------|--------------|
| 8 | Perfect | 0% |
| 15 | Good | 10% |
| 20 | Need to reread | 25% |
| 25 | Difficult | 35% |

But you shouldn't write only eight-word sentences. That makes your writing boring and very repetitive. You need to change length to avoid monotony. (Do you see what I have done here?)

If you want to cut words, there are four techniques that give you easy wins.

### → Make a conscious decision to cut your adverbs.

These are words that modify verbs, and they're often a sign of inexact language. Instead of 'Alex Soutar walked slowly and confidently', change the verb: 'Alex Soutar strolled.' Let the verb do the work. Your audience will appreciate the effort you make to find fresh and original verbs.

### → Use the passive voice sparingly.

When you write 'The plate was broken by Valeria' rather than 'Valeria broke the plate', you need more words, so readability immediately worsens.

### → Choose everyday language over bizspeak.

Speaking and writing like a human will make it easier for you to connect with other humans. This sounds obvious, but many writers and presenters get panicked and fear they come across as unprofessional if they use everyday language. They don't. Instead, avoiding bizspeak will dramatically increase your ability to connect. If you have the choice, always say 'Buy your tea from the guy with the trolley' rather than 'Customers can purchase refreshments from the onboard catering assistant.'

→ **Cut out redundant words.**

We know every dilemma is a difficult dilemma, so there's no need to state it. Here's a small selection of phrases that can be halved without any loss of meaning.

| Bizspeak | Humanspeak |
| --- | --- |
| advance planning | planning |
| end result | result |
| new innovation | innovation |
| past history | history |
| sudden impulse | impulse |
| unexpected surprise | surprise |

Now you're aware of how common these redundancies are, you'll see and hear similar empty phrases all the time.

# The bizspeak bandit

**Sadly, you'll come across bizspeak at the exact moment when a company should be at its most human.**

An absolute classic is presenting joiners with a company mission statement – or even a *vision statement*, if you're feeling particularly pretentious – that's so vague as to be meaningless. The laws of libel mean I can't share the worst with you, but I've designed a one-armed bandit that does the job. Pull the handle and the machine will give you the help you need to complete the phrase 'Our mission is to ...':

Here's what I got on my first attempt:

'Our mission is to <u>globally</u> <u>embrace</u> <u>user-centric</u> <u>consumer experience</u>.'

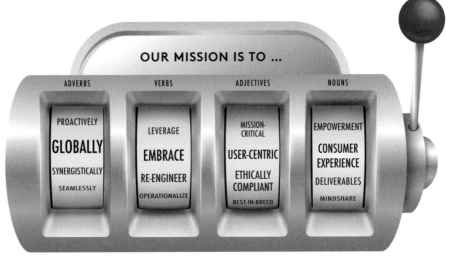

Your turn. Pull the lever and see what you create:

**Our mission is to ...**

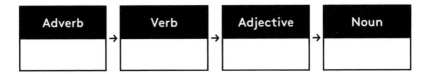

| Adverb | | Verb | | Adjective | | Noun |
|--------|--|------|--|-----------|--|------|
| → | | → | | → | | |

Do you see how easy it is to produce a sentence that sounds important but is actually meaningless? Sadly, we've become so accustomed to this guff that we accept it as normal.

# Some mission statements are good!

## I've been scathing about the vocabulary and yawn-inducing message of most vision statements.

But some are precise and motivational. The following examples are masterpieces of concise, FAB-focused writing:

**Honest Tea** (US): 'To create and promote great-tasting, healthy, organic beverages.' It's clear and short, and there's an extra half-mark for the pun on 'honesty'.

**Budget** (New Zealand): 'We will consistently deliver a quality product, friendly service and great value that make customers confident that Budget is their best car rental choice.' Wordy but clear, with a focus on why the customer would choose them in a very competitive market.

**Care** (Egypt): 'CARE works around the globe to save lives, defeat poverty and achieve social justice.' Strong verbs such as 'defeat' and 'achieve' make you feel you are in the company of determined, decisive people.

But sadly, most mission statements sound as though they've been run through faulty translation software a few times. Here's one that always used to irritate me: 'LOT Polish Airlines, in an innovative and effective way, is prepared to meet the needs of today's international traveller, both leisure and corporate flyers alike.'[3]

---

3    I'm especially keen on including LOT's verbose and clumsy statement after their errors left me stranded in Warsaw and they refused to refund my tickets.

## Where to Next?

→ To follow up these themes, look at:

- Chapter 9: Apply what you've learned in this chapter to the story frameworks. Why not be brave and speak one of your stories out loud?

- Chapter 14: More tips on words to choose and words to avoid in this chapter on writing style.

- Chapter 17: What memorable opening lines have stuck with you? 'Last night I dreamt I went to Manderley again,' perhaps, or 'Like you, I prefer short intros.'

# CHAPTER 5

# Removing the barriers to communication

You are responsible for your communication. Any gaps between you and your listeners will disappear when you identify the obstacles.

## A communication barrier can arise every time a message is sent

**A barrier is any factor that stops the right meaning from being communicated.**

There are many causes of interference, but they all have the same result – the message you want to transmit is *not* properly received by your intended audience.

## There are many ways communication can go wrong

**I'm jotting down notes in a waiting room high above London Bridge station. A flash of winter sun streams through the windows and bathes the room in red light.**

Red? Why red? Because the shelves are stacked high with red files. Patients' names are written on the files' spines in many different hands. Some files are bundled together with thick elastic bands. What hells must a patient have been through to rack up three thick files of consultation notes and X-rays during their life?

Doctors, nurses, porters, administrators and directors need to talk to each other about complicated subjects in the minimum of time and with maximum accuracy. Then they must explain bad news and difficult decisions to very ill patients and their petrified loved ones.

Hospitals are complex organisms. I think of them as hives where the bees speak different languages. What could possibly go wrong?

→ **Words change their meaning when they're used by different groups.**

When a nurse tells a doctor that a patient has suffered an 'insult', he's using medical jargon for any illness or accident that's caused serious damage to a limb or organ. But when the same nurse uses this technical term to a patient – 'Your right leg has suffered an insult' – it causes confusion, and maybe even some sniggering.[1]

## → Emotions are everywhere.

I can get panicked when I talk to doctors. They're the smartest kids from school, the ones who studied hardest at university. They grew up to dedicate their lives to saving people, while I spend my finest hours getting drunk with poets.

I don't want to display my ignorance by asking 'dumb questions' ('When you say "short term", do you mean three days or five years?'). I know my doctor is always busy, so I won't waste her time by asking for clarification of terms such as 'aggressive' and 'benign'. If I don't know the difference between a negative and a positive test result, that's my fault, right?

What a patient wants to hear also affects their experience. Dr Joy may be popular with patients precisely because he finds it hard to break bad news. Phrases such as 'little problem' or 'We'll do our best' may give a vulnerable patient a false sense of optimism. Dr De'Ath's honesty – 'There's nothing we can do to save him' – may stop people from listening to him.

## → Institutions have their own rules about communicating.

These may be formal policies ('Shift handover cannot last more than 15 minutes') or 'habits' that are never questioned (using slide decks rather than emails to share information).

## → Many hospital conversations are unbalanced.

Doctors are often revered by patients, who may be afraid to challenge them or ask for more information. Experienced nurses assume that junior doctors have more practical and theoretical knowledge than they do. Technicians may under-report problems to senior management because the messenger with bad news is rarely rewarded. Managers may be afraid to confront doctors who misreport the cause of death of

---

[1]    This gets much worse when medical staff inadvertently reveal the secret language they share: 'frequent flyer' for a hypochondriac, 'departure lounge' for the geriatric ward and (my all-time favourite) 'Velcros' for family members who overstay their welcome.

a patient with co-morbidities (which is medical jargon for 'more than one illness or disease at the same time').

## → Everyone is different, unfortunately.

Our past experiences colour our communications. Physiological factors play a part. Without realizing, an anaesthetist may rush through a consent form with someone who has poor hearing. The patient's reading glasses might be in a locker outside the operating theatre. Everyone who works in a hospital is exhausted, and that combination of poor sleep and vital decisions may mean they choose speed over checking comprehension.

In a corner I see a doctor explaining patiently to three adult women that their mother has to be kept in overnight after she collapsed in dialysis. Their body language suggests that they have plenty of questions, but the doctor's pager beeps and – understandably – he snatches it from his pocket. The daughters talk and he nods but he's hearing without listening. They're not happy, but he's needed in transplant surgery immediately.

## → The micro-environment always has an impact.

Did you visit a hospital during the Covid-19 pandemic? They are frantic places at the best of times, but in March and April 2020 in Europe they were basically war zones. A friend of mine worked a 53-hour shift. Just imagine how hard it was for her to issue instructions and listen to helpers, to read emails and keep records, when she'd not stopped running from one emergency to another for more than two days. At a less dramatic level, a hot waiting room makes people sleepy and inattentive while a freezing-cold consultant's office makes us eager to leave.

Looking around, I see the incipient signs of PTSD in the team around me. I'm a visitor, relatively healthy, and my main concern is that the cafeteria will close before I'm finished. They, by contrast, are exhausted, uncertain, stressed and shell-shocked. While I'm choosing between cappuccino and caffè latte, they have to make life-or-death[2] decisions about which patient receives a scarce resource and which doesn't.

---

2     An overused phrase, I concede, but 100 per cent accurate here.

→ **Any illness weakens our mental functions.**

Patients can't process new information, and can't plan. Thinking in sequence, especially if conditionality is involved, is almost impossible for patients who are very ill. The sentence 'If the first operation isn't successful, you'll have two different treatment paths to follow' is an unsolvable problem to anyone who's spent days without good-quality sleep. The effects of Long Covid include fatigue and depression. When combined with deteriorating cognition, they create the toughest conditions for communicating I've ever seen.

# It's your choice to communicate in a simpler way

**There's a world of difference between spoken and written communication. The method you choose is a trade-off between Richness and Spread.**

→ **Rich communication**

The richer the method, the more personal it is. A face-to-face conversation allows back-and-forth dialogue and is good for discussing subjects that are complex, disturbing or sensitive. When someone asks in an email 'Shall we have a call about this?', they want to share a richer means of communication.

Rich conversations – which could be scheduled meetings or an informal chat in the corridor – allow us to display emotional nuances that don't come across in a group Zoom. The listener is more aware of our body language (a defensive crossing of the arms over the chest, an open stance) and senses fluctuations in our tone of voice. But rich methods demand time and energy. When you commit to listening to the person in front of you, you can't communicate with anyone else.

→ **High-spread communication**

People publish reports because they're a great way to share ideas and information with a wide audience. You can include graphs and images, which is difficult in a face-to-face conversation.

But the wide spread of such communication means it is very easy to ignore. Just think how many reports you've downloaded to read later, and then immediately forgotten about.

Technology allows us to send our message to millions of people at the touch of a button. The problem is that methods of high-spread communication are normally very low in richness. It's easy to ignore yet another message flicking up on the Year 6 Lost Uniform WhatsApp group.

| Richness | The way you communicate | Spread |
|:---:|:---:|:---:|
| ↑ | Planned face-to-face conversation<br><br>Standing-up chat in the corridor<br><br>Tailored storytelling presentation<br><br>Phone call<br><br>FaceTime, Skype<br><br>Zoom<br><br>Personal text<br><br>WhatsApp group message<br><br>Group email<br><br>Report<br><br>Article or blog post | ↓ |

Here's the trade-off. The richer the conversation, the fewer people you can reach. The greater the spread, the more people you can reach but the less impact you'll have on each one.

# Active communicators get through all the barriers

**I've concentrated on communication problems in this chapter, until now. Many speakers aren't aware of these barriers until it's too late.**

But there's no need to be pessimistic, because there are many ways to improve the way you send your message.

→ **Return to FAB.** Remind yourself of what Feelings, Actions or Beliefs you want to change. Return to the *why* of the communication to keep your focus.

→ **Take responsibility for your message.** It's too easy to blame external conditions for communications that fail. I've spoken to groups for whom English was the third language, worked with deaf people on interactive storytelling and delivered a lecture series on business writing in a room above a curry house. (Not, thankfully, all at the same time.) Sure, conditions could have been better, but it was down to me to adapt to the audience and situation.

→ **Work hard to create better conditions for richer communications.** Find a physical space where you can talk one to one without interruption. Acknowledge that your listeners (and you) may be tired, stressed or worried about the news you're sharing. Disconnect from as much technology as possible, because we are all overloaded. Be prepared to have a break or even postpone if your listener shows signs of fatigue.

→ **Name the communication problem.** There's no shame in saying you can't hear the Zoom call because there's too much background noise. Raise the problem early to get it solved quickly. We often feel embarrassed to point out others' technological glitches, especially if we feel our listener is above us in a hierarchy. But remember, the more senior a person, the less time they have to waste on poor-quality communication.

→ **Sharpen up your vocabulary.** We can adapt the Flesch method we saw in Chapter 4 to spoken communication. The same rules apply. Keep sentences short and punchy. Choose short words instead of protracted and obfuscating circumlocutions. Avoid redundant phrases and jargon as much as you can.

→ **Check for understanding.** You can ask individuals for proof of understanding. Simple questions – 'Do you see what I mean?'; 'Is that clear to you?' – are OK, but people tend to say 'Yes' automatically, for fear of looking stupid. A smarter way is to ask your listener for a summary of what you've told them, or how your news will affect them.

→ **Invite people to ask questions.** Listen carefully, for questions often reveal what you haven't communicated clearly.

## Where to Next?

→ To follow up these themes, look at:

- Chapter 3: Return to the four micro-stories you wrote. What barriers might crop up when you tell them?

- Chapter 11: Lots of the tips on voice are directly applicable to spoken conversations.

- Chapter 15: Giving and receiving feedback is fraught with emotion. Read this chapter and imagine how our personal responses may become a barrier to communication.

→ Take a look around you. Wherever you are reading this, identify the barriers to communication. They exist in libraries as well as airports, online and IRL. Awareness of barriers is the first step to removing them.

# PART 2

# How to Bui a Stor

ld

y

# CHAPTER 6

# Make structure your superpower

Your favourite books and films rely on surprisingly similar structures. Once you understand how stories are built, you'll become a much more confident writer.

# The best stories are built with invisible structures

**The word 'structure' is a double-edged sword. It implies strength and solid foundations, which are undoubtedly good things, but it also hints at an unattractive rigidity. When we hear phrases like 'the rules of story construction' we feel that creativity is under threat.**

I invite you to think differently. Structure means form, but that doesn't necessarily mean formulaic. Guidelines are essential if an audience is to follow your story, but they don't limit your imagination or your ambition. They're derived from thousands of years of storytelling, and are as relevant to the ancient Hindu epic *Mahabharata* as they are to *The Sims 4*.

Storytelling structure must be flexible as well as strong. Sometimes a home built from bamboo is better than one made from bricks.

# Focus on Situation, Complication and Resolution

**What use are conflict and struggle if they don't change the hero? The structure of Situation, Complication, Resolution has stood us in good stead since the days before papyrus was popular. Let's take a look at one of Aesop's *Fables* to see how Situation, Complication, Resolution makes the story flow.**

A steaming-hot day on the lavender-scented slopes of Mount Olympus. A solitary crow has got used to quenching his thirst from a narrow terracotta jar abandoned years ago by a sleepy shepherd. But today the heat has evaporated much of the water that drips into the jar from a waterfall. The crow, dying of thirst, tries to get to the bottom of the jar, but his beak isn't long enough.

What does he do to stay alive? He drops a single pebble into the jar. Almost imperceptibly the water rises. He drops another pebble, then another, and within an hour the cooling water has risen to the top of the jar.

| Situation | Complication | Resolution |
|-----------|--------------|------------|
| The Hero ... | ... encounters an obstacle ... | ... that transforms them. |
| A crow ... | ... is dying of thirst ... | ... but he learns how to survive. |

How is the crow transformed? He's survived his physical ordeal, which was his priority. But he's also learned that intelligence can overcome problems, that necessity is the mother of invention, and that winners never quit. (It always surprises me just how many different morals people can take from fables.)

The Situation, Complication, Resolution structure is ubiquitous in movies. It works equally well in romances set in rural France, comedies set in coke-fuelled Wall Street and noir-tinged 1940s thrillers.

### → *Chocolat,* directed by Lasse Hallström, 2000

Situation: The vivacious Vianne Rocher opens her chocolate shop in Lansquenet-sous-Tannes, deep in rural France, just as the staid and religious villagers begin Lent.

Complication: Vianne argues with the town's pompous mayor and makes friends and enemies with aplomb. When a band of Roma arrive on the outskirts of town, Vianne falls for the handsome, charismatic Roux. But the couple – and Vianne's shop – are viciously attacked.

Resolution: Despite the risks, Vianne conquers her constant urge to uproot her life. She learns that patience and stability are as valuable as her secret recipe for lust-inducing white chocolate truffles.

### → *Working Girl,* directed by Mike Nichols, 1988

Situation: Tess McGill, a working-class secretary who takes business studies at night school, has one last shot after being sacked from her Wall Street job.

**Above, left:** *Chocolat*: 'It's not easy being different.'
**Above, right:** *Working Girl*: 'I have a head for business and a bod for sin.'
**Left:** *Mildred Pierce*: 'I never used to drink at all. It's just a little habit I picked up from men.'

Complication: Her new boss, the ice-cold Katharine Parker, steals her ideas. Tess falls for Katharine's partner, Jack Trainer. When Tess and Jack start working together, Katharine schemes to crush her.

Resolution: Tess survives, and shows Jack that Katharine is manipulative. Tess is promoted. She will be a much better boss than Katharine.

### → *Mildred Pierce*, **directed by Michael Curtiz, 1945**

Situation: The hard-working and entrepreneurial Mildred supports her family by baking cakes and pies. Her brattish daughter, Veda, disapproves.

Complication: Mildred works as a waitress, sets up her own restaurant and is soon heading a chain of diners. Veda becomes a lounge singer and blackmailer. She murders Mildred's second husband.

Resolution: Mildred realizes that money cannot buy happiness. Furs and diamonds are worthless when your daughter doesn't love you.

What's the thread shared by these three stories about three very different women in three different places and times? Their responses to Situation, Complication, Resolution transform them into heroes.

# What do we mean by transformation?

**There are many ways a character can be transformed in a story. They can slay their personal dragon, survive the battle or finally find the love they always desired.**

Harry Potter gains enough confidence to take on Voldemort. Neither Thelma nor Louise can face returning to her old life. In no more than three strides and the lighting of a cigarette, Roger 'Verbal' Kint becomes the feared Keyser Söze.

If nothing changes in your hero – and I do regard Verbal as the hero of *The Usual Suspects* – you won't make an emotional connection with the audience. Without transformation, you've got *Seinfeld*. The show's lead writer, Larry David, was against transformation because he wanted to show that the characters were forever stuck in their unchanging world. Famously, he told the other writers and the show's actors that the series would have 'no learning, no hugging'.[1]

One technique you can adapt from scriptwriters is to start with the end scene very clear in your mind. Focus on the message you want your audience to leave with when your tale is finished. What single idea do you want them to remember? Now double-check that your hero's transformation shows the value of this idea.

# Expanding your structure into three acts

**Syd Field could tell a winner from a loser. None of the nine screenplays he wrote ever made it to the silver screen, but his job as a script assessor for major studios turned him into the guru of Hollywood scriptwriting.**

---

[1]    Just to be clear, *Seinfeld* is my favourite comedy series ever. The episode where a coffee-table book about coffee tables opens into a coffee table is one of the funniest twenty minutes I've ever seen.

He distilled his learning into books and courses; his book *Screenplay: The Foundations of Screenwriting* (1979) sold more than a million copies and has been translated into over forty languages.

Field read up to 1,000 scripts a year, but recommended only 2 per cent for further consideration. He found that too many scriptwriters forgot the basics of a beginning, a middle and an end. So he invented the Syd Field Paradigm, with its three acts, which became a classic storytelling structure.

| The Syd Field Three-Act Paradigm | | |
|---|---|---|
| Act 1 | Situation | We meet a hero and learn about the world where the story will take place. |
| Act 2a | Complications | The tension rises as the hero faces obstacle after obstacle. |
| Act 2b | More complications | Field splits his second act into two parts. This signifies that Act 2 is twice the length of Act 1 or Act 3. |
| Act 3 | Resolution | The final act resolves the story. The hero is transformed (by victory or by defeat) before returning to his original world. |

Field's Paradigm is vintage wine in a sleek new bottle. It adapts classic elements of mythic storytelling for the silver screen.

In between the three acts you'll find plot points. These are decisions, events or characters that send the story in a new direction.

## → Plot Point 1

This occurs when the hero commits to the quest. Juno decides to give her baby up for adoption; 007 collects his new toys from Q and heads off in search of the villain.

### → The Midpoint

The most important plot point usually happens exactly halfway through Act 2. In *Walk the Line* (2005), June Carter (the real hero of this Johnny Cash biopic) sleeps with the country singer for the first time. In *Bonnie and Clyde* (1967), the couple become triple murderers.

The midpoint reveals information to the hero (or the audience) that fundamentally changes the direction of the movie. Or there's a sudden reversal of fortune that brings a massive obstacle. Nothing will be the same after this. If you ever feel a movie drags after about 50 minutes, it may be that the midpoint is weak or non-existent. On the other hand, a dramatic midpoint makes the audience hang on your every word. In the four-part TV adaptation (2005) of Sarah Waters's *Fingersmith*, the midpoint occurs at the end of the second episode. It's a great switch, more surprising than most twist-in-the-tale endings, and will leave you breathless.

### → Plot Point 2

This is where the hero is at their lowest. They're surrounded by baddies, up to their neck in quicksand or circled by hungry sharks that have scented their blood. We can't see how they will survive, but they must or there won't be an Act 3.

*The Silence of the Lambs* (1991) mixes adrenaline-filled horror with layers of deep psychological insight. It's the elusive, perfect mix: a twisty story that keeps you glued to your seat, and that you can't stop thinking about for weeks afterwards. It follows the three-act structure to the letter.

Remember what I said about invisible structures? I was so engrossed by *The Silence of the Lambs* that I watched it four times before the three acts and the plot points revealed themselves to me (see chart opposite). An audience notices structure only when it's missing.

| The Syd Field Three-act Paradigm | | |
|---|---|---|
| Act 1 | Situation | Young FBI recruit Clarice Starling is picked out of her FBI Academy class to interview Hannibal Lecter, a notorious serial killer. |
| Plot Point 1 | | *Lecter offers Clarice a deal: he will write a profile of a killer called Buffalo Bill in exchange for a move away from the Baltimore Asylum.* |
| Act 2a | Complications | The FBI offers a fake deal to Lecter. He enjoys taunting Clarice. |
| Mid-point | | *Catherine Martin, daughter of a senator, has been kidnapped by Buffalo Bill. Lecter will help, but only if he's flown to Tennessee to talk to the senator face to face.* |
| Act 2b | More complications | The FBI believe they are closing in on Buffalo Bill, but their SWAT team is at the wrong address. Buffalo Bill tries to capture Clarice. |
| Plot Point 2 | | *Lecter escapes!* |
| Act 3 | Resolution | Clarice kills Buffalo Bill. She returns to the FBI Academy. Confident, wise beyond her years and battle-hardened, Clarice is now Agent Starling. |

# Structure improves your presentations

## Time for some Netflix and learn. Here are five ways you can become the Alfred Hitchcock of the Share Screen world.

→ **Take your structure from the movies.**

Make sure your hero begins in a Situation, faces a Complication and is transformed by a Resolution. No one's asking for a fully fleshed-out three-act structure, but your presentation must have a clear start, middle and end.

### → Make an emotional connection.

A CEO who tries to persuade you with facts and graphs immediately creates two problems. Firstly, her audience will seek to reject her argument on an intellectual level. They'll be sceptical about her facts and critical of her numbers. Before she's uttered a word, people are searching for holes in her theory. We are rarely moved to action by reason on its own. Experience trumps evidence every time.

The second problem is the lack of emotional connection. It's the difference between handing out information about how much land you farm and giving people a bowl of juicy strawberries and thick cream produced on that land. We remember an experience forever, but bullet points are forgotten before you've even switched to the next slide.

### → Provide inspiration.

Reports and stories are different. We use reports to disseminate information and our opinions. Their tone of voice is authoritative, perhaps a little dry, which fits the content – data, statistics, evidence, findings, surveys and summaries. The fixed structure of a report can't be changed once it's printed.

Storytelling is about connecting and inspiring. The content – journeys, quests, villains and conquests – should be dramatic and exciting. When delivering live, you can curtail sections that make your audience yawn or expand on areas that excite them.

### → Create an impact.

Humans love stories and humans love music. But I can't pick up a guitar and play a gig without learning chords and practising for hours. You can't tell a story without investing in your skills. If business storytelling was easy, we'd all be great at it.

Storytelling forces you to use parts of your brain that have lain dormant for years. It's more effort than pressing Ctrl/C and Ctrl/V on a report until it sort of fits on a slide. But it is the most effective way to persuade people to change. And it's fun, too.

### → Finish with a cliffhanger.

Imagine you're finishing a story in front of a packed room. The crowd are cheering, your team are on their feet, even your dry-as-dust director is whooping. But a nagging doubt you've had during the presentation has now formed itself into a question: 'If I'm not the hero of this story, who is?'
The answer will be revealed in the next chapter.

## Where to Next?

→ To follow up these themes, look at:

- Chapter 10: Reread the short section on dilemma. How you can build a dilemma into your next story?

- Chapter 16: You'll see that *The Silence of the Lambs* really got under my skin. Find out how pathos creates emotional connection, even with a duplicitous, manipulative cannibal.

- Chapter 19: Headlines and subheads give structure to a report.

→ Do this. Re-watch a favourite movie and identify the three acts and the plot points. You might be wary, fearing that your new knowledge will weaken the magic of the filmmaker's art. Don't worry, because the opposite will happen. Knowing about structure will increase your enjoyment.

# CHAPTER 7

# We can all be heroes

You might forget the plot of a book, but you'll always remember the hero. If you want to connect with the audience's emotions, you must show the hero's transformation.

# A hero without a journey is like a cowboy without a horse

**The Hero's Journey transforms an ordinary Joe or Josephine into a winner. The journey and its steps were codified by the writer Joseph Campbell (1904–1987), an expert in both myth and psychology.**

Campbell analysed stories from around the world and found that they followed very similar patterns. There's a fantastic revelation about storytelling on every page of *The Hero with a Thousand Faces* (1949), but no one wishes the book was longer.

It's possible to map the twelve stages of the Hero's Journey to Syd Field's Three-act Paradigm. A caveat before we delve deeper. I've only got six pages to summarize the life's work of Field and Campbell. I can't do justice to the nuances of their wisdom, but I can present you with a guide that you can use immediately. And I want you to remember that any structure is a framework, not a straitjacket. As a storyteller you have the freedom to adapt these structures.

Shall we begin?

# A great storyteller takes the audience on a journey

**Why do so many presentations fail? You knew some of the answers before you read my book: they're boring, the presenters are frightened or arrogant, there's no engagement or emotional connection.**

You, however, are different. You know that storytelling makes a deep emotional connection with an audience. And, by now, you realize the importance of structure to storytelling. Presentations that lack a story pattern are doomed to fail. Stealing some structural elements from *Booksmart* or ancient Norse myths will make your ideas come alive.

Imagine you are giving a training course to thirty people. It doesn't matter what the topic is, or where you are. I've used the story approach to train in subjects as diverse as bond maths and creative writing in Kuala Lumpur, Mexico City, Cairo and – something of a career highlight – a power station near Dartford in the Thames Estuary. In all these places I've used the Hero's Journey and the three-act structure to influence the FAB of my delegates.

Always remember that structures are flexible. Never feel obliged to jam all the elements into your story. I recommend that you concentrate on six elements of the hero's journey to entice your audience:

→ **Element 1: Your audience begins in their Ordinary World.** They'll shuffle into the hall, or yawn as they click on Zoom, unaware that their mundane lives will never be the same again. You have a responsibility to give them new skills and eye-opening insights. You've lived in the Special World, that place where you slew dragons and conquered mountains, and they all want a piece of your action. Even if they don't yet know it.

Statistics vary, but it seems you've got no more than eight seconds to make a positive impression on your audience before they zone out. Use those seconds well.

→ **Element 2: The call to adventure.** Training creates lasting change when it moves a person from ignorance to knowledge. To get buy-in from your listeners, it's important to establish what holds them back. Without getting into the torturous jargon of 'training needs analysis' and 'unconscious incompetence', you must contrast where they are now with where they could be after spending time with you.

One storytelling technique that works well here is to highlight the difference between the hero's ordinary world and the special world they are about to enter. If the challenge is worthwhile, the listener should feel resistance. There has to be enough at stake for them to feel scared about failing.

The audience needs to cross the **dramatic gap** themselves. It's far better to encourage them with the promise of personal transformation than to kick off with a bland list of bullet-pointed objectives.

| Now – the ordinary world | The Dramatic Gap | Future – the special world |
|---|---|---|
| Hero is static. | We create tension through the contrast between yesterday (frustrated, bored, unhappy, underskilled) and tomorrow (excited, different, happy, skilled). | Hero is transformed. |

→ **Element 3: Meet a mentor.** A good trainer has to balance their ego against the needs of the audience. You should be confident, happy in your abilities and a big enough personality to fill the room with your energy or command the Zoom with your digital presence. But you must also avoid being a dick.

An honest mentor makes clear the difficulties ahead. There will be tests, challenges, moments when giving up seems the most attractive option. But the satisfaction of finishing the course, passing the exam or getting the certificate will be worth it.

→ **Element 4: Engagement is guaranteed when they cross the threshold.** When I'm teaching, I'm always conscious of that moment when the whole class becomes committed. Delegates I've taught before or who have read my books are with me from the first moment.[1] Others are more sceptical. They'll sit with their arms folded across their chest, or slump back in their chair, needing to be convinced. But there comes a moment – usually when a micro-story proves my worth to them or they all laugh in recognition at one of my office disaster stories – when the whole class gets it. I scan the room or my computer screen and everyone is concentrating, heads forward and eyes on me.

People cross the threshold only when they have chosen to get involved. No amount of bullying or sloganeering gets their commitment. You, as their mentor, can take them to the edge

---

1    It would be wrong of me to use the word 'always' in this sentence.

of the cliff, but it's up to them to jump off it to the secret beach paradise in Thailand.

Most people like the thought of personal transformation, but the pain of change stops them from taking action. Your job is to motivate them out of the comfort zone. Many of us are happy with the status quo, but, to quote the cruel music teacher in *Whiplash*, 'There are no two words in the English language more harmful than "good job".' You're the mentor, and a gifted mentor inspires people to be more than good enough.

→ **Element 5: Facing the ordeal creates a world of contrasts.**
Your audience's journey will be up and down, backwards and forwards, impossible and then pretty easy. They will feel the buzz of positive emotions such as anticipation and determination, before falling into bouts of sadness and anxious uncertainty. They zoom up, crash down, feel fear in their stomach and shout out in exhilaration. And then they do it all again because they enjoy the rollercoaster of emotions you have created.

Complications should become more extreme the deeper you get into your teaching. Cases and content need to get harder to keep them engaged. The last hurdle must be the hardest one to clear.

→ **Element 6: The heroes in your audience will be changed by their journey.** You will have changed the audience's knowledge of your subject. And you will have changed the audience's knowledge of themselves.

Training can be exhausting, but when I finish teaching a course I often notice that delegates leave with renewed vigour and an increased sense of purpose. They've accepted – and completed – a challenge, and that's something that will change them. One transformation will lead to another.

→ **The hero's inward journey reflects their outward journey.**

The hero's journey is visible externally. We marvel as Wolverine fights in wars for 100 years, gasp as the diver is hugged at the end of *My Octopus Teacher*, cry when Catherine Earnshaw dies just after giving birth in *Wuthering Heights*. But it's their internal journey that excites us most.

# The storyteller is not the hero

**I'm at a networking event where I already know most people in the room. A tall man introduces himself and launches into a story about how he left home for the US as a 16-year-old to seek his fortune. He did well, rising effortlessly to the top of the corporate pile and retiring at 50 on a pension that's more than I earn. How do I know? Because he told me exactly how much he gets.**

He doesn't ask me anything about myself. Instead, he talks about his many and varied successes. He launches into his retirement plans: a tech start-up, a lecture tour, maybe there's a book inside him.

I leave for some prawn and avocado canapés that I neither need nor want. I pass the tall man on my return from the buffet. He's buttonholed a friend of mine who works at IE Business School. He's telling her about how he left home for the US as a 16-year-old to seek his fortune ...

I watch the tall man for the next fifteen minutes. He's slick, confident, happy to mingle and eager to hand out his business cards. But he's as boring as watching paint dry. Hell, he's as boring as watching grass dry. He walks up to my friend from the business school. I watch her face fall in terror. I earwig. He's telling her the same story for the second time.

The tall man shows no interest in other people and can't even fake listening skills. He may as well wear a badge saying 'It's all about me.' He's missed the whole point of storytelling.

It's not about you, it's about the audience.

→ **You are the mentor, not the protagonist.**

Your job is to point the way and help the hero overcome obstacles. The structures we've looked at exist to help you be the storyteller. They're not designed to show off your personal greatness.

Most mentors have been heroes in the past. You are valued for your experience and skills and also – crucially – for your ability to tell your story. People choose a mentor who inspires and stretches them, whose wisdom will guide them towards success. They want an expert, but one who shares. Humility is a very attractive attribute in a world full of bragging.

*A teacher is never a giver of truth;*
*he is a guide, a pointer to the truth that*
*each student must find for himself.*
Bruce Lee

# At last! The shock ending I promised in Chapter 6

**Every person in your audience is their own hero.**

I freely concede that this is not as powerful as 'Luke, I am your father,' but once you understand it, business storytelling becomes much, much easier.[2]

## Where to Next?

→ To follow up these themes, look at:

- Chapter 2: Take another look at Elizabeth Holmes. Can you see how she made her life story fit the Hero's Journey?

- Chapter 9: We'll go through some classic examples of business storytelling. When you do the exercises, be conscious of the moment of transformation.

→ <u>Think about this.</u> Some novelists will tell you that middles are much harder to write than beginnings or endings. Take a book that you found unputdownable and work out why the hero was so important to you.

---

2    This is actually a misquotation. When I set out to write *The Story Is Everything* I made a vow not to mention *Star Wars*, because every book on storytelling talks about it at such jaw-dropping length. For the record, I think it's an OK movie, but other films are available.

# CHAPTER 8

# Creativity hides in plain sight

Myths about creativity can hold you back. But once you understand how the creative mind really works, the ideas will pour out of you.

# The truth about your brain ...

**The cerebrum is the largest part of the human brain. It's divided into two hemispheres. Thankfully, neuroscientists avoid complex technical vocabulary and label these halves simply left and right.**

We are indebted to the American neuropsychologist Roger Sperry (1913–1994) for showing us how the cerebrum is split. Sperry won the Nobel Prize in Physiology in 1981 and is proof of the benefits of studying widely. His first degree was in English, his masters was in psychology and his doctorate in zoology.

→ **The left side loves business, academia and intellectual pursuits.**

It's all about words and numbers. It's the part of your brain that writes To Do lists and crunches stats. Critics see the left side as inflexible and overly analytical.

→ **The right side is more artistic and imaginative.**

It writes songs and weaves colourful costumes, it sees the world in 3D and has great spatial awareness. Its detractors regard the right side as emotional and illogical.

Sperry's research took place over two decades. It's detailed, scientific and rigorously tested. He'd be shocked – and maybe even a little ashamed – to see how his conclusions have been twisted into one of the most reductive ideas in popular psychology.

His most pertinent quotation is not about the divide between the two hemispheres, but about their union:

> *It's important to remember that the two hemispheres in the normal intact brain tend regularly to function closely together as a unit.*
> Roger Sperry

# ... And the myths about your brain

**Too many books and YouTube videos propagate the myth of the left- and right-brained person. This false divide leads to the extremely limiting assumption that either people are creative or they are not. That's a dangerous lie. Those who believe this meta-myth see the left brain as a drag on the creative right brain.**

The English poet Ted Hughes considers this in 'The Thought-Fox', which appeared in his first collection, published in 1957. It's an amazing poem about inspiration. While studying English literature at Cambridge, Hughes went to bed at three in the morning because he was unable to finish an essay. In a dream a terrifying fox, as tall as a man and with burning skin, rakes a human-shaped hand over Hughes's essay. The fox warns Hughes that if he continues writing for academics his poetic spirit will die.

We're all worried about our own personal thought-fox. How do we combine the two sides of the brain into business (left brain) and storytelling (right brain), when everyone tells us they are separate?

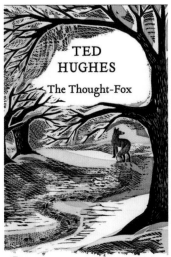

Probably the only thing I have in common with Ted Hughes is a gnawing fear of 'this blank page where my fingers move'.

The meta-myth takes a subtle twist when we think about organization and structure. Some right-brain-dominant people are secretly jealous of the skills and attributes of the left-brainers. The left-brainers effortlessly meet deadlines, keep their studios tidy, plan ahead and work in a logical, controlled manner. They set up cool websites to sell the things they've made, and get their taxes done on time.

→ **The left and right sides are part of the same brain.**

Which belong to the same human. They're not split by an impenetrable wall but linked by the corpus callosum, full of the white matter that allows communication between the two hemispheres. We need both sides to work well and talk to each other if we are to flourish and grow as human beings.

# Ways to turn on your creativity

One of the most overused words in business is 'creative'. I've been asked for 'creative solutions', had many a long lunch with cabals of 'creative consultants', and even been asked to join a 'creativity circle' at an investment bank where I worked. What's ironic is that mentioning the word 'creativity' always kills originality and imagination stone dead.

You must give creativity some love to make it appear. We are all naturally creative, but many of us have hidden our creativity, especially at work. Twenty years after we last wrote a story for fun, we're baffled when we can't get the words to flow on command. The natural creativity we had as children – when a cardboard box became a dolls' house and a garden was an entire empire – is still with us, buried and a little rusty like an old spade forgotten under sand. A polish and a clean are all it needs to shine again.

# Let's play, as one kid says to another

I'd like to share five techniques that will get the creative genie to leap out of the magic lamp.

### → <u>Pretend to be someone different.</u>

What would happen if your story had a different narrator? This isn't an invitation to take a four-year course in Stanislavski Method Acting, but a simple change to the narrator's point of view.

Acting as someone from a different country or era will allow a markedly different approach. Switching gender, or finding a place between genders, will most definitely change the cultural assumptions of the storyteller. Thinking yourself into someone else's shoes always leads to a massive change in voice.

### → <u>Become a child again.</u>

Children are proud of what they create, but they're very rarely precious. They know their lovely sandcastle will be washed away by the tide, so they pick up the shells and use them on the next one. When you watch children playing, it's easy to see that their imaginations are unlimited. Fun, original and awe-inspiring ideas spring up without the use of the office whiteboard. Crazy, I know! So buy some sweets for your inner child and let them play.

> *Look at life with the eyes of a child.*
> Henri Matisse

### → <u>Copy without producing fakes.</u>

Sometimes I advise novelists and poets to write in a particular style: the romantic give and take of Sally Rooney, or the terseness of Ernest Hemingway. I ask them to copy out a paragraph by a favourite author and then change words – nouns, an adjective, then a verb – to produce something entirely new that still has echoes of a successful writer.

Do this with pen and paper, rather than computer, to get a more visceral connection with the writing and your ideal author. You'll fill the empty page in no time with original text while learning the rhythm of another writer. As you imitate more you'll write more; you won't produce an exact copy, and in those gaps between your author and you a new voice will magically appear.

Another technique is to write a summary of a plot that

really grabbed you. Once you map out the twists, turns and timescale in *The Great Swindle* (2013) by Pierre Lemaitre or *A Fatal Inversion* (1987) by Barbara Vine, you'll understand how brilliant these two authors are at structure.

Don't be afraid to emulate. Leonardo, El Greco and Rubens started as apprentices, and they all seem to have done well by learning their craft from a master.

> *If I have seen further, it is by standing upon the shoulders of giants.*
> Isaac Newton

## → We're all better in the morning.

Working late is OK if you've got a life-or-death deadline to meet, but it saps your energy. The next morning you'll be shattered and stale. Don't ever work late through choice – even the most dedicated night owl knows this is a poor move.

When you're asleep, your unconscious mind will continue working on your story. You won't be aware of this, but neither are you aware that the waves are still lapping the shore while you're dozing in a deckchair. Your mind may dream up a new character or some snappy lines. Solutions to problems crop up. And even if the midnight muse doesn't appear to you, a good night's sleep will help. You'll see things in a clearer light in the morning.

## → Find more time to do nothing.

One temptation you must resist is the urge to create stories 24/7. Creativity drains us. I never write for more than three hours a day, because I like being fresh and relaxed. My perception of time got seriously skewed during the second lockdown of 2020. Some days passed in seconds, but an afternoon of Zoom calls seemed to last a month. I heard tale after tale of friends burning out through overwork or lack of work, getting stressed because they had too much or too little on their To Do lists.

Whatever you call it – mindfulness, zoning out – make sure you have time every day to switch off. Meditation is a smart way to replenish and rejuvenate. I suggest you take a course at a reputable yoga centre rather than online, because there's power in group meditation. If that's not your thing, just sit somewhere you feel safe and relax as many muscles as you can. (I always begin with the muscles at the side of my jaw, which is where I store a lot of tension.) Lighten and lengthen your breathing. If it's appropriate, close your eyes and become aware of the noises around you. Start off with a minute, and no more. Tomorrow you'll want to do two.

## Where to Next?

→ To follow up these themes, look at:

- Chapter 2: Go back to the financial adverts. Can you create better, sharper ideas for the FABs?

- Chapter 13: Find the exercise called 'The Joy of the Blank Page'. It teaches you just how easy it is to write.

- Chapter 15: It's common to think of responding to feedback as a mechanical activity. But smart writers use the final polish to add creativity.

→ Imagine this. You are the hero of a favourite book or film. How have your feelings, actions and beliefs changed by the time you reach the end?

# CHAPTER 9

# Classic stories to have in your back pocket

You'll be more confident once you've got these three stories prepared. So, enough of theory – let's get creative!

# It's time to write

**I bet you're a great storyteller. You've seen plenty of examples and learned the theory in earlier chapters, but, as we near the halfway point of *The Story Is Everything*, you'll be itching to write.**

But first, an important distinction. You can tell **stories about yourself**. These are perfect for interviews and to show friends how you accomplished a task or smashed through a mental block. Your story about personal growth or disaster will reveal what you are like at work.

You can also tell **stories about your organization**. It may be about that time you went the extra mile for a disabled customer or how your ethics were tested by a lucrative dam project that might have damaged the environment. In some cases – for entrepreneurs monetizing their hobby, for example – the distinction will disappear. Your story about working will reveal who you are as a person.

This is a good time to share three writing tips that I've picked up from very different parts of my life.

1. My maternal grandmother came from Zurich and always used to tell my mum '*Taten sagen mehr als Worte*.' This translates as 'Actions speak louder than words', an exhortation to tell stories about how fabulous you are, but only if they are true.

2. I had a not very good boss at PricewaterhouseCoopers who kept telling the whole department to 'walk the walk before we talk the talk'. In her own clumsy, clichéd way she was giving the same message as my grandmother, albeit in a 1980s power suit.

3. Every book or course on creative writing is legally obliged to use the phrase 'Show, don't tell.' Thankfully, I've managed to shoehorn it into this paragraph.

A reminder before you dive in. Mindset is an important part of storytelling confidence. Human beings have always told stories to connect with others. You are part of a conversation that's been happening for many thousands of years. Listening to stories is hardwired into human existence;

the audience is waiting for you to give them something unexpected, informative and fun.

So far, so theoretical. Now it's time to consider the practicalities of writing three types of story. We start with a Dramatic Gap story about personal transformation. Then we look at an attention-grabbing story structure that explains why people set up a company (or why you're planning to start one). We finish off with a simple technique to show how you improve customers' lives. Ready?

# <u>Story 1:</u>
# What you learned by overcoming an obstacle

**Interviewing people for a job is interesting for about 20 minutes, but after three consecutive days of 'My greatest fault is modesty' it becomes hard to distinguish between one candidate and another.**

To counteract the boredom, I always ask people to tell me about a time when they faced adversity. I pay attention to how they tell their tale and I'm fascinated by what they've learned from the experience. I'm looking for a variation on the Dramatic Gap we saw in Chapter 7.

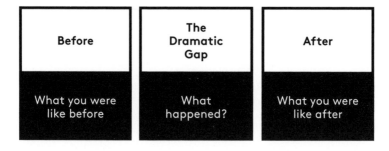

My favourite example is 'Arthur's Transformation', which you can find on YouTube. Arthur Boorman is a paratrooper who damaged his knees so badly that he had to use a cane, leg braces and finally a wheelchair. When a doctor told him he'd

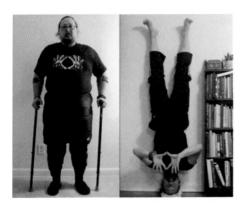

Arthur Boorman has earned
the right to show off.

never walk normally again, Arthur gorged his way to 135 kilos
and prepared to die young.

Diamond Dallas Page, an ex-professional wrestler, teaches
yoga online. Arthur bought a subscription to his course and
followed his advice. The video shows Arthur's excruciatingly
slow progress – the falls, the fails, the bangs into the wall, the
earthquake-sized tumbles to the floor. Every wobbly balance,
ungainly stretch and sweaty mistake is captured by an
unforgiving camera.

But then, miraculously, Arthur takes his first tentative
steps. He casts aside his walking stick and starts to jog. At
the end of the video he's running.

It's an emotional video, which appeals to universal themes
such as personal growth and making positive decisions in our
lives. You'll cry when you watch it, I promise. Diamond Dallas
Page is smart because he doesn't make the story about him
or his product. Instead it's all about the impact his product
had on an individual. Arthur Boorman, clearly, is the hero of
this story.

### → Stories are the one place where conflict is encouraged.

A hero needs to struggle, so make sure they face at least one
strong opposing force. Conflict could be internal ('Arthur has
given up on life at the beginning'), external ('Repeated
landings on military exercises have destroyed Arthur's knees')

or 'villainous' ('More than one doctor told Arthur to give up and accept his fate'). The more obstacles your hero has to face, the less certain the end of the story. Cliffhangers arouse the emotions of the audience because we're all desperate to find out what happens next. This is one video you won't switch off halfway through.

Your turn now. Think of a time you overcame a problem. Write words or phrases that describe each of the three phrases in the boxes below. You can write two sentences if you like. Don't worry about being perfect, just get the words down on the page.

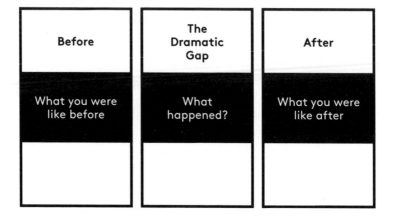

# Story 2:
# Foundation story

Most cultures and religions in the world have a creation myth.[1] The Old Testament says that God created the world in six days, the Koran says it took Allah six *youm*. The ancient Greeks believed that Gaia (Mother Earth) turned the chaos of nothingness into life, while in Chinese mythology Pangu cracked an egg to release Yin and Yang, who formed the sky and the Earth.

---

1      An interesting exception is Buddhists, who believe in the concept of beginningless time.

Corporates also have their own foundation stories. For many years Pam Wesley, the founder of eBay, told the world that the company began when her fiancé built her a website so that she could trade her collection of Pez sweet dispensers. Wesley found an appreciative audience for a story that combined human elements: a woman with a kooky hobby, the strangely romantic gift of a free website, an accidental business that grew to take over the world. But it was a *myth* dreamed up to make the real story – an efficient marketplace for online transactions – more personable. Storytelling skills, rather than a business plan chock-full of process flow charts, distinguished eBay from its many competitors in the mid-1990s.

## → What is a myth?

In common usage, 'myth' means a story that is untrue or even ridiculous. But for theologians and anthropologists, myths are stories a culture invents to explain and spread its sense of identity. Myths say more about a race – or a company – than the truth ever can. Does lying about its beginnings harm a company? In the case of eBay – and also Google, Facebook and YouTube – the answer is an emphatic no.

## → Creation myths follow a set structure.

It doesn't matter if they're about a world egg containing two sets of twins or how the first tweet was sent. These stories always have structural elements in common.

The world begins in a primordial state. It's wind and chaos, and Wi-Fi hasn't even been invented. Then the deities arrive, bringing their power, wisdom, skill, experience and tremendous drive. Creation is a conscious and planned act. Like a great business plan, the path to market domination is clear. The actions of the deities show both their freedom (they have decided to launch their new product) and their power (they know the launch will succeed). They create a paradise, then populate it with animals and eventually humans. Everything is fine until Adam eats the apple or the CEO is found plotting murder in Belize.

| 1 | Primordial State | Before us, there was nothing. |
|---|---|---|
| 2 | Supreme Being(s) | I/We bring power, brains, skills ... |
| 3 | Conscious Creation | Definite plan. |
| 4 | The Reasons for Creation | Freedom and power. |
| 5 | Paradise | Perfect world. |

## → Why invent a corporate creation myth?

Corporate creation myths are great when you need an *encapsulation* for rapid communication. They're used when a founder is in full-on networking mode: spieling the elevator pitch to a venture capitalist, or recruiting talent to join the team. The best myths combine an individual's passion ('I read four books a week') with a corporate vision ('People pay a premium for a curated reading list'). But the mistake many people make is to interpret the myth as fact rather than as a well-crafted, often-repeated short story.

The creation myth is very different from the overcoming an obstacle story you've just written. You don't talk about the products that failed, the trials that ended in disaster, the law cases you lost and the intellectual property you stole. Sheer luck, which is part of every business's success, is never mentioned. You stay silent about the colleagues who left and the friendships you broke. The creation myth sets a tone for the company when you first meet people, but don't get high on your own supply and start to believe it.

## → Use the five-stage structure to create your myth.

I want you to write a corporate creation myth, using the five stages we've talked about. If you're involved in – or planning

– a start-up, this will be easy to write. If you're not currently working, write about a company you would love to start. If you're working for a company that isn't yours, speak to people about its origins. Every big company has a story about how it was formed, even if, ultimately, it's a myth.

| 1 | What was the market like before you entered? | |
|---|---|---|
| 2 | What did you (and any partners) bring to the company? What was it that made you stand out? | |
| 3 | What convinced you that there was a market for your product or service? | |
| 4 | What did you want to achieve? | |
| 5 | What was the impact of your creation on the market? | |

# Story 3:
# This is what we do, and this is why we do it

**In the mid-1990s I worked for an investment bank.
One of the partners had just heard about a mysterious
new technology called the internet.**

He sent me a document full of buzzy business phrases such as 'empowerment through networks' and 'simultaneous client/server interactivity'. I had no idea what he was talking about (neither did he, obviously), but that night I went to have a beer with a friend who'd just joined one of the UK's first dotcoms.

Emma's office near Old Street was a converted warehouse on the fringes of the cheapest part of the City of London. I felt 100 years old in my suit and tie, while all around me people wore jeans and T-shirts with ironic slogans. A new group called Oasis blasted out of the CD player.

Emma was glued to the screen of her Apple Mac. 'Shh. I'm just finishing a game of Monopoly with my new girlfriend.'

'OK,' I said. Alarm bells were ringing.

'Yep. Now we've got the information superhighway, the only problem is the time difference.'

'Eh?'

'She's in Okinawa.'

I knew the partner's document, with its straplines 'digital inclusion' and 'welcome to the world of digital connectivity', was as old-fashioned as my highly polished black brogues. Emma had taught me what the internet was all about in a ten-second conversation.

→ **What you do becomes important only when it connects to the client's FAB.**

Scroll forward twenty-five years, and I'm assessing funding applications for a business-school incubator in Madrid. I've been brought in to look at the final shortlist of ten. There's a lot at stake for the applicants – they'll get free office space, valuable connections and free consultancy. Some may even get an investment of equity capital, a commodity that has been thin on the ground since the recession took hold.

I reject four start-ups in less time than Emma took to put a couple of houses on the prime real estate of Park Lane. Why? I'm looking for a two-line explanation of what they do and why they do it. If their reason to exist doesn't leap off the page and smack me in the face, I file them under 'Forget'.

Avoid all that pompous business-speak about values and brand culture. I'm not interested in your previous struggles. You and your company are not my heroes. The only person I care about when I pay for an app, gig tickets or groceries is me. Show me how you will transform me, and I'm suddenly interested.

Always return to FAB. Let's consider a pair of shorts from the American company Lululemon. I have a friend, Ruth, who was a brand ambassador for their sportswear and gave me a pair of their shorts during the most depressing days of lockdown. It sounds bizarre, but I'm convinced those shorts helped me to get fit! They changed the way I felt about myself and what I did to take care of my body. And they certainly transformed what I think about premium-price sportswear.

|  | Before I had them | After I had them |
|---|---|---|
| Feelings | Stiff, unfit, weak, sluggish | Energetic, powerful, flexible. |
| Actions | Sit on sofa and get fat. | Go to yoga and sweat it out. |
| Beliefs | Gym gear can't change you. | £80 for a pair of shorts is a bargain. |

→ **Focus on the client's transformation.**

You've probably already guessed the last task on your list. Fill in the boxes below, describing a buyer of your product or service before and after they buy it. Make sure you concentrate on the client, not your company. Remember, we may need a spirit guide to show us the way and an antagonist to make us grow, but we are all the heroes of our own story.

|  | Before I had them | After I had them |
|---|---|---|
| **Feelings** |  |  |
| **Actions** |  |  |
| **Beliefs** |  |  |

# Where to Next?

→ To follow up these themes, look at:

- Chapter 11: Stories about overcoming obstacles are most effective when delivered in an appropriate voice. What are the characteristics of that voice?

- Chapter 19: Use these tips on headlines to ensure your story starts with a bang. Or at least an attentive audience.

→ Think about this. Consultants often talk about a brand 'speaking' to a customer. Go for a walk around your home. What brands – food, drink, clothes, technology – have successfully spoken to you over the years?

# CHAPTER 10

# The elements of amazing storytelling

God is in the details. Listeners love stories that are crafted with skill and care. The elements you'll read about in this chapter will ensure that you – and your story – are remembered for all the right reasons.

# You can learn from all the great storytelling that surrounds us

Can you hear the murderous music that plays whenever a shark attack is imminent in *Jaws*?[1] Do you remember Meg Ryan, er, enjoying her sandwich during the 'I'll have what she's having' scene in *When Harry Met Sally*? What about the Alien bursting out of John Hurt's chest, 'La Marseillaise' being sung in *Casablanca*, the moribund house of the ghost-like Miss Havisham in *Great Expectations*?

Love comes in many forms. Harry to Sally, 'I love that you are the last person I want to talk to before I go to sleep at night' (left); Miss Havisham to Estelle, 'Break their hearts and have no mercy' (right).

In this chapter I'll give you examples from adverts, films and novels. Think of these as the sprinkles of cinnamon or vanilla that make your coffee magical. They are practical storytelling techniques to boost the quality of your writing.

## Conflicts are vital, but dilemmas are better

Conflict is not always hero against villain. Sometimes it can come from the hero fighting against something inside her, or even against the whole world. Jane Eyre is torn

---

1  I'm going to mention *Jaws* three times in this chapter. Steven Spielberg's blockbuster made a huge impression on me. It was the first 18-plus movie I sneaked into, and frankly I was too young for it.

**between her desire to be loved by a man and her wish to keep her independence, but she's also a poor and unconnected orphan struggling against the rules and hypocrisy of her society.**

Conflict is vital for stories. It adds uncertainty to the hero's journey, so the audience wants to know what happens next. Conflict makes us root for the hero, which creates the emotional connection we need to read the next 400 pages of Stieg Larsson or watch series 5 of *Better Call Saul* in one night.

Dilemmas raise the stakes even higher. A dilemma occurs when a character has to choose between two options, both of which come with a significant downside.

The relationship between a parent and a child can be fraught with dilemmas. In *Gone Baby Gone* (2007), the detective Patrick Kenzie must choose between following the letter of the law (bringing a kidnapped young girl back to her mother) and letting her grow up in a far more supportive and comfortable environment. We stare open-mouthed as the unnamed hero in Bong Joon-ho's *Mother* (2009) stretches the definition of what a good mother does to protect her son. And in *Sophie's Choice* (1982), Zofia Zawistowski faces the heartbreaking decision between losing her son or her daughter.

Dilemmas are great in business fiction because they force the hero into a corner. Their resourcefulness and convictions are tested: does a bond dealer sacrifice her own ethics to help a client in trouble; can a third way be found between the rock and the hard place?

We've focused a lot on heroes, so it's important that villains don't escape our attention. Make your opponent worthy of your hero. You build a three-dimensional antagonist by explaining their motivation – are they desperate for market share, or righting a perceived wrong, or fighting for their own cause? Don't make them an ogre who just likes doing bad things. They must exist in their own right and as a foil to the hero. Acknowledge their importance to the story. Without Moriarty, Sherlock Holmes is just a fading detective with a penchant for Class As.

# Use all the senses

**Specific details create images in people's minds. Vivid details give you credibility because they convince the audience that you were there. It's this authenticity that helps you build rapport with your audience.**

Imagery fires the imagination. Sight is the dominant sense for most people around the world; we tend to interpret the world primarily through our eyes. Details give an 'I was there' veracity to your storytelling. Good authors plant strong visuals in the audience's brains. Great storytellers appeal to all the senses. Add at least one of these to your story to make it come alive.

→ **Taste.** Have you ever come across a menu engineer? These are catering psychologists who work to increase sales and margins at restaurants. They look at design and pricing, but spend a lot of time on descriptions. We cringe at clichés like 'mouth-wateringly irresistible' and 'locally sourced', but the right words do get us salivating. And salivating customers tend to be less picky about price. One successful technique is to 'humanize' the taste. That's why you read 'Grandma's secret recipe for coq au vin' or 'Cider made from apples picked in the Garden of England'. Check your palate. Are these descriptions working?

Kilgore is on screen for only 11 minutes of *Apocalypse Now*, but his impact lasts well beyond the final scene.

→ **Smell.** War is what keeps Lieutenant Colonel Bill Kilgore in *Apocalypse Now* (1979) happy. His wistful phrase 'I love the smell of Napalm in the morning' sums up the career soldier better than 500 words of backstory. Smell is a strong component of memory – remember your first classroom or the smell of frangipani that evening in Koh Phangan – so use it to evoke the past.

→ **Touch.** I hate touching suede, unvarnished wood or hair that's no longer attached to its owner. (I'm not going to tell you what I love touching at this early stage in our relationship.) Touching is a very acute sense that promotes strong reactions in listeners. Use it more.

→ **Sound.** When the shark-hunter Quint scratches his nails across the blackboard in *Jaws* the whole room (and the whole cinema) pays attention. It's a great way to show that he isn't afraid to rile people to get their attention.

The hunter Quint has a knack when it comes to terrifying people: 'This shark, swallow you whole. Little shakin', little tenderizin', an' down you go.'

Henry Hill in *Goodfellas*: 'To me being a gangster was better than being the President of the United States.'

# Start quickly

**Avoid the storyteller equivalent of clearing your throat in public. You're not a Victorian novelist with twenty pages to describe the storm clouds gathering over the Wessex countryside. This is especially true when introducing yourself to your audience.**

Consider these three examples:

'My name is Henry, I've been in catering for twenty years ...' Stop!

'I'm so happy to have been invited to speak at ...' Stop!

'As far back as I can remember, I always wanted to be a gangster ...' Go!

Henry Hill, the protagonist of *Goodfellas* (1990), doesn't mention his stakeholders, his key performance indicators or his passion for the more informal parts of the hospitality industry.

Ditch the corporate and conventional in favour of story. Begin the story with the real you, not your LinkedIn profile. (In Chapter 16 we talk about establishing your credibility with the audience, but that's very different from boring them with a long introduction. Dive in, and they will follow.)

# Take people on an emotional journey

**A story that is solely comprised of low moments (failure of a product launch, being taken over by a penny-pinching private equity fund) will be depressing. But a story that is all high moments (a brand conquers a continent, a successful strategy is implemented without problem) will also be unbearable.**

Stories need tension and release, ups and downs, darkness and light ... well, you get the picture.

→ **Being the hero of our own life is a vital element of the human psyche.**

Once you realize that every single member of your audience is on their own personal journey, your storytelling changes.

Customers will always care more about their story than about yours.

This has huge implications if you're talking about a brand or product. Don't waste your breath telling people how great you are. Instead, make the client your hero and tell them how your gym supplement or tax advice will help them achieve their goals.

→ **The hero's return shows us that learning has taken place.**

They have been changed by their time in the unfamiliar world; the skills and attributes they learned there are much more apparent now they are back home. My favourite real-life example of a successful return is a friend from school who joined the pilot training scheme in the Royal Navy. He arrived at speech day in a huge, bright yellow rescue helicopter, which he landed on the school cricket pitch.

Shared experiences are a great way to connect with the audience. We have all been a scared child or a newbie in their first job. Whether it was in Oslo or Osaka, in 1943 or this week, the feelings will be the same. Finding common ground with your listeners will always endear you to them.

# Keep it simple

**It is very unlikely that anyone will ever ask you to make your presentation longer or more complex. Be aware of the time constraints of others.**

This is especially true online, where the rejection statistics are brutal. Your customers must now be able to tell what you do the moment they reach your website.

Human beings, as we saw in Chapter 3, are always looking for shortcuts. We're bombarded with information and hounded by adverts every second of the day. A company that helps a consumer cut through noise with a sharply constructed message will always do well.

You and DIY? Trust them, it's going to be fine.

### → <u>Short sentences can convey great meaning.</u>

Ronseal gives us a genius example in eight words: 'Does exactly what it says on the tin'. The phrase positions the products as unintimidating, reliable and simple to use. The company acknowledges that not everyone painting a fence this weekend is an expert builder. But as heroes in our own story, we like the feeling of making a better home for ourselves and our loved ones. We will choose products that help this happen.

'Does exactly what it says on the tin' strikes a big chord. It's moved from the advert into everyday usage to describe things – a holiday hotel, a style of politics – that are reliable and honest. There's even a song by Katie Melua called 'What It Says on the Tin'. I suspect, however, that the lyrics were inspired more by the vast number of words that rhyme with tin – bin, sin, begin, win – than by any profound love of DIY.

Humour can be a risky strategy, but when it works the results are phenomenal.

### → <u>Create a clear message.</u>

Audiences love to summarize. *West Side Story* is *Romeo and Juliet* in 1950s New York, *Alien* is *Jaws* in space, *Snakes on a Plane* is, well, snakes on a plane.

Can you provide the audience with a single message, clear and unequivocal, that they could pass on to their friends? And can you do it without lecturing or preaching?

You may have created the best product or service the world has ever seen, but no one gives a damn unless you can communicate the benefits you offer to the consumer. Too much business storytelling is about the company rather than the consumer. I don't care about a company's share price or that its logistics hub is in Seville, but I do want to know how spending my hard-earned money will make me feel better.

Your message must be simple and relevant. It's got to be something one happy customer can tell another.

The Hans Brinker budget hotel in Amsterdam pokes fun at itself with slogans such as 'Same hotel lots of new complaints' and 'Now even more noise'. But these self-deprecating messages are perfect for its target market – young, slightly stoned backpackers on a tight budget who don't care about minibars or a turndown service. These are messages that the hotel's demographic enjoy sharing online and in bars.

→ **<u>Messages about loss are effective.</u>**

We often frame what's at stake in terms of what a listener can gain. Flip it round, and you can focus on what the audience or customer will lose if they're not successful. John McClane in *Die Hard* (1988) has to foil the terrorists, but his true motivation is to avoid his own death. He's not Rambo or the Terminator, just a man who wants to patch things up over Christmas with his estranged wife.

People are often motivated to avoid loss more than they are by gain. Try this test. Imagine how bad you would feel if you lost one million euros from your back pocket. Take some seconds to feel the pain, fear, anxiety and sadness. Now imagine what you would feel if you found a million. Elation, joy and happiness would all be in the mix. But would the good feelings outweigh the bad? For most people, they won't.

Telling clients what they can miss out on is an effective, if occasionally dangerous, tactic. I recommend that if you mention failure (the loss) you make it clear how you can help people avoid it (and gain success).

# Be you

**This chapter has given you lots of advice, practical tips and hints on mindset. But it's vital to avoid anything that makes you feel phony or fake.**

Keep what works for you, chuck what doesn't. If a suggestion doesn't chime with you, ignore it. There'll be another one along in a minute.

*Facts are up to 22 times more memorable*
*when presented in the form of a story.*
Jerome Bruner, cognitive psychologist

The default setting of the human brain is story. I can't stress this enough. Humans love stories and they want to enjoy listening to you tell yours. An audience will prefer a nervous speaker who tells a tale over a super-slick presenter who rattles through one slide after another.

Remember what your presentations used to be like? Lights, camera, painfully dull slide deck? The yawns and snores of your late-afternoon audience? Thankfully, those days are over.

## Where to Next?

→ **Parts 3 and 4, of course.**

# PART 3

# How a Fant a Fant Storyt

to Be

astic

eller

# CHAPTER 11

# Finding your storytelling voice

Nailing down your storytelling voice takes time and effort, but it will make you a unique presenter. Analyse your favourite influencers, speakers and writers for inspiration.

# Voice is a paradox

**A unique voice makes you stand out in a world jammed full of content and noise, but try too hard and you will come across as bogus. We separate our personal and professional selves at work, but readers and listeners demand us to be authentic.**

A further contradiction is that a successful voice depends on both consistency and change. Fans and followers will love you because they recognize your style from the first words of the podcast or the opening paragraph of your article. But your voice will develop the more you speak.

The final paradox is that to sound natural you need to craft your voice. It's like handwriting – no one is born with it but over the years you develop your own style. It takes years of practice, hundreds of thousands of written words and a ton of rehearsals and presentations before you feel comfortable. So, cut yourself some slack if you haven't got it perfect just yet. Your voice has to be constructed to make it sound real.

*The key to success is sincerity.*
*If you can fake that you've got it made.*
Attributed to American comedian George Burns,
French novelist Hippolyte Jean Giraudoux and
English stand-up Frankie Howerd

# Three steps to establish your voice

**You need to take just three steps to establish your voice as a writer and presenter.**

→ <u>**Step 1 is defining how you want to come across.**</u>

Overleaf is a list of 25 words that describe storytellers. Circle the ones that apply to you and feel free to write down any that I haven't listed. (Please don't do that self-help book thing where you glance at exercises without doing them. I really want you to do this task.) Try to end up with a list of five words.

| | | | | |
|---|---|---|---|---|
| Authoritative | Fun | Outspoken | Angry | Philosophical |
| Smart | Inspiring | Playful | Organized | Sharing |
| Emotional | Sarcastic | Witty | Clever | Logical |
| Intellectual | Gentle | Generous | Sincere | Detached |
| Curious | Awestruck | Passionate | Cynical | Impartial |

You can also write down words that aren't on the list

.........................................................................................................

.........................................................................................................

→ **Step 2 requires feedback from your listeners and readers.**

What are the adjectives they use to describe your voice? It's great when there's lots of overlap between these first two stages. It's great when there's a lot of overlap between how you want to come across and how people perceive you.

It's more common, however, to identify mismatches. There's a problem if you think you're a 'charming mix of funny and provocative' but your audience sees you as 'serious and well-balanced'. If this divergence occurs, you need to do some more work on voice.

A mistake at this stage is to try to appeal to as many people as possible. To be successful, you have to accept another voice paradox. The more a podcaster visualizes one reader, and the more he speaks directly to her, the more listeners believe that podcaster is speaking directly to them. To get a large audience, you have to focus specifically on one person. Ashto and Jonesy of the 'What You Will Learn' podcast may have thousands of followers, but it always feels as though they are talking only to you when they're recommending books.

When I prepare my work, I always imagine the same listener, Clare, sitting in the chair opposite me. She's a smart person, but not an expert in my subject. She has high standards when it comes to grammar, logic and presentation, but she's also supportive and forgives my mistakes. If I keep Clare in her chair just through my words, I know I'm on the right track. But if she grimaces at certain words or phrases, I know that my voice is wrong.

→ **Step 3 considers the writers and presenters you like.**

There's no point lying now just to impress me. I freely concede that *The Simpsons* is more of an influence on how I write than Dostoyevsky is. We aspire to be the people we admire, so work out what it is in a voice that appeals to you. You'll find there are a lot of factors to consider.

Make a list of five authors and presenters you like. Throw a wide net! Next to each name, write five positive adjectives about that person. I'll do it with five of my faves:

George Orwell: clear, honest, direct, influential, experienced
John le Carré: impassioned, complex, dramatic, thoughtful, driven
Kate Atkinson: wise, surprising, prepared, funny, observant
Jonathan Meades: driven, academic, surprising, intelligent, honest
Marcus Aurelius: erudite, detailed, understanding, knowledgeable, thorough

What does my list tell me? That I like people who are clever but who can use humour to make a point. That I trust people who have done their homework, and can't stand those who make things up on the spot. That I like to hear the voice of real experience and that I can spot a bluffer a mile away.

What does your list tell you? Take a look at the adjectives and find common themes; maybe emotional appeals work well for you, or you prefer the serious and sober to the excited and passionate. I'm not advocating that you copy them, but you will find techniques and attitudes to 'model' until you find your true voice. As storytellers – and as people – we are the sum of our influences.

# Many factors change your voice when you're presenting

**Think back to FAB and re-consider your objective. There's a difference between frightening people into immediate action ('Stop flying now to save the environment') and convincing them that climate change is real ('The evidence shows the Arctic sea ice is shrinking 13 per cent every decade').**

It's good to be clear about your personal and professional objectives when it comes to voice. Your voice will be different if you want a long-term relationship with the audience or if you have one chance to shock them out of their skins.

As we consider each factor, remember presentations where the speaker has followed these guidelines. They'll be the successful ones!

→ **Adapt to the audience.** Reading people's faces will tell you whether your voice should become simpler or more complex. (Please don't judge my judging. I'm only making explicit the processes that all public speakers go through if they care about their audience.)

Make the presentation *simpler* when: they are beginners in the subject matter; there's little time; they're inexperienced and in the early stages of their education.

Make the presentation *more complex* when: they are experts in the subject matter; there's plenty of time; they have lots of experience and are highly educated.

Your voice will adjust – consciously or unconsciously – because of factors such as the audience's clothing (modern or traditional), industry (creative or analytical), interaction (friendly or cold), and even their chatter before you talk (friendly or formal) and their body language (open or closed).

→ **Unique personal perspective.** Perhaps you've spent thirty years at Saatchi & Saatchi or maybe you worked 24/7 during Uber's start-up. Whether you come across as wise or irrelevant, a new broom or an aggressive upstart, will largely depend on the voice you choose. Our life experiences give us a unique vantage point.

→ **Structure.** You may lead your audience on a linear journey from inciting incident to final resolution, or you may be a discursive speaker who pulls several strands together to reach a definitive conclusion. You'll also adapt your voice to the 'logistics' of the presentation; you'll need a very different approach for a five-minute chat with three people than for a one-month course for fifty thousand followers on Domestika.

→ **Words are vital.** So vital, in fact, that I've devoted the whole of Chapter 14 to how word choice affects your style.

Please remember that your voice is always a work in progress. Eventually you'll write a story or deliver a punchline that could only be you. That'll be the moment you find your voice, but you will never stop changing it.

## Voice and speaking are not the same

### We often feel there's a gap between what's in our head and what's on the page or screen.

When you listen to a recording of an unscripted conversation, you'll hear interruptions, mistakes, mispronounced words and long periods of silence. Questions go unanswered, ideas are repeated. Speaking is natural and is normally spontaneous. Writing is different. It's planned, revised and corrected. (Well, at least, it should be.)

We criticize ourselves because we have to work hard at something we feel should be organic and easy. But this struggle is part of the beauty of creativity. It's because it demands effort and skill that it becomes worthwhile. Don't fall for the myth that voice is unprepared and unplanned. You need to work at this. Here are three practical ways to bridge that gap between your idea and your voice.

### → <u>Record yourself.</u>

When writing hurts worse than toothache, a voice recorder is a relatively painless way to shape a first draft of your ideas. It's especially good for storytelling because it allows you to practise the voices of your different characters. Recording makes you sound more authentic, and that's absolutely crucial for building rapport with your listeners.

Recording is also a great way to boost your productivity. It feels better to delete 100 recorded words than 100 written words. Once I'm happy with my recording I copy it into Word or, if I'm feeling lucky, I'll chance my arm and use dictation software. I change anything that sounds terrible and delete bits that are long-winded or repetitive. In ten minutes I get a rough draft that would have taken me an hour to write.

### → <u>Imagine someone else playing you in a movie.</u>

Mentally hand your script to one of your favourite actors. The imagined peer pressure from Robert De Niro or Daisy Edgar-Jones will raise your game. I also walk around as I talk, trying different approaches and structures as I search for the appropriate elements that make up my voice. I know that my voice will come across more clearly this way than if I was struggling with words on a page.

### → <u>Adapt as you present.</u>

Magically, it's sometimes easy to find your voice *during* a presentation. I know many academics who write four-page sentences and impenetrable footnotes yet who are great at explaining their subject over a pint in the college bar. A good storyteller will change the cadence and style as she becomes more familiar with the audience.

Changes in intonation give you great flexibility. Body language offers many ways – from the micro-expressions on your face to the flailings of your arms and legs – to nuance your message. Your audience wants you to succeed. When you see entertained and engaged faces in front of you, you know you've found your voice.

## Where to Next?

→ To follow up these themes, look at:

- Chapter 16: The interplay between word choice (an aspect of logos) and pathos (the ability to connect emotionally with your audience).

- Chapter 17: Reread some books that had a major impact on you. You might not remember the plot or the characters' names, but I bet you'll remember the voice. If you're short of inspiration, try *To Kill a Mockingbird* (1960) by Harper Lee, *Jane Eyre* (1847) by Charlotte Brontë and Emma Cline's *The Girls* (2016).

→ <u>Think about this.</u> Listen to a favourite cast and work out how the presenter's voice grabs you. Use the five adjectives method to analyse their voice.

# CHAPTER 12

# What is flow, and why does it feel so damn good?

Flow happens when your ability and the difficulty of your task are matched. A task that's too easy will bore you, but a task that's too hard will destroy your confidence. Find the sweet spot and you'll get your flow on.

## What does flow feel like?

**Flow – like love – is all around us. It's the feeling you get when you're immersed in your task.**

You hear it when a guitarist on stage improvises the perfect solo, and you see it when a child spends a whole afternoon playing with Lego. People in flow radiate a marvellous energy: they're focused while enjoying every second of painting their masterpiece or cooking up a feast.

It's easy to enter into flow during physical activities. A 10km coast walk around Margate can pass in seconds once you've found your rhythm, but if your boots don't fit it will feel like hours of hell. A yoga class is a joy if your mind and body are in union; wear the wrong pants and it will feel like 24 hours of sweat and pain. It's exactly the same with storytelling. Once you find your flow state your stories appear without stress and you'll love what you're doing.

It's rare that we can definitively state that a concept was discovered by a single person. But the systematic study of flow, and its popularity as a mindset in sport, business and the arts, must be credited to Mihaly Csikszentmihalyi.[1] People have adapted his ideas for their own ends (as I'm rather doing here), but no one has ever expressed the idea of flow better than him: 'an automatic, effortless, yet highly focused state of consciousness'.

You know you're in flow because it feels great. You're engaged and your skills are developing. Flow is performance-enhancing rather than being a struggle. You don't get distracted by noise or by other people, even if you're in a busy rehearsal room or creative studio. You're hyper-focused and there's something trancey about the whole trip. In the words of Noël Coward, 'Work is more fun than fun.'

---

1     His surname is pronounced *Chick-Sent-Me-High*, more or less. In the same way that my surname is pronounced *Loo-ee-zoo*, more or less.

# How to find your flow

→ **<u>Flow is about matching your ability to the degree of challenge.</u>**

We plot *challenge* on the vertical axis on the left of the chart below. This starts at easy (a WhatsApp message to your five-a-side football team) and rises to very difficult (that ten-volume memoir of your life that's been in the pipeline since you were a teenager).

We plot *ability* on the horizontal axis. Start at the left with low ability (absolute beginner who can barely write a sentence) and move towards the right until you arrive at high ability (towering literary genius).

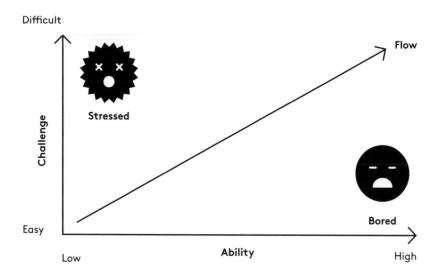

→ **<u>You'll get stressed if the job is too hard.</u>**

In this example we ask a very inexperienced writer to produce a 1,000-word article on a subject she doesn't know anything about. And, to make it worse, we give her a 20-minute deadline.

What happens? Her mind freezes, her body tenses, she can't write a word. The mismatch between high challenge and low ability creates terrifying stress. And stress, as we all know, is the mortal enemy of creativity.

### → You'll get bored if the job is too easy.

Too easy is also a deterrent to flow. We now ask a very experienced writer to come up with a story about her company's sustainability policy.

This is the fifth year she's written about the environmental footprint of the company and, rather lazily, she's just going to revise the piece she submitted last year. It'll be OK, nothing special, and she'll be bored writing it. Her lack of enthusiasm and originality will be sensed by her readers.

### → You'll find flow when the job and your ability are matched.

We're all looking for a task that stretches us but doesn't leave us destroyed. The challenge has to be enough to develop us as a human being. We like the sense of achievement the job gives us, and this gives us the confidence to approach slightly more difficult tasks. A similar principle is at the heart of video-game design – we want level 9 of *BioShock* to be a bit harder than level 8, but not so much that we abandon the game as impossible.

Flow doesn't happen without your involvement. You have to take responsibility for tackling more demanding tasks and improving your skills via courses, mentoring and wonderful books like this one. But once you commit to growth, the flow channel widens. You become someone who craves a creative challenge.

Being in the flow state is a wonderful feeling. You'll have hundreds of original ideas and your creativity will blossom. Writing becomes fun and painless. You'll want to write – and present – more.

# Flow starts with motivation ...

**Why are you writing? Your motives could be external, internal or a mixture of the two.**

→ **External motivation gives you a short-term push.**

You'll write more when you need to pay the rent or escape a prison sentence. Exams and tests make us focus. But external pressure never makes us love a topic.

→ **Internal motivation is more powerful.**

You invent stories because you're in love with the characters and want to know what happens to them. You tell tales to convince the listeners of the rightness of your argument and the moral worth of your point of view. You enjoy frightening an audience, or making them laugh out loud, just with the power of your words.

# ... And grows with preparation

**You can't turn on flow with the flick of a switch. But there are steps you can take to access it. You don't need to do all these, so see what works for you.**

→ **Warm up your writing muscles.** Don't dive in cold, but play a little with words before you start in earnest. Can you rewrite a sentence in your company's annual report using alliteration or avoiding the letter 'e'?

→ **Have clear objectives.** You need to be definite about why you're practising your speech. Remind yourself of your FAB and what you want to change. If your objectives are muddy or too numerous, flow will elude you.

→ **Focus on the pleasure.** Forget about word count, at least for the moment. Forget about the audience, because now you are imagining stories for your own enjoyment. Forget about editors and reviewers, because this is for you.

→ **Be mindful.** Twenty minutes of uninterrupted creativity will bring you more joy than an entire day of flipping between Facebook, Insta and your dating apps. And twenty minutes of meditation and quiet time will open up your imagination to new ideas and ways of expression. Go on, see if you can live without Wi-Fi for an hour.

→ **Get your shit together.** Don't start without your laptop, pens, chewing gum, paper, reading glasses, snacks or whatever it is you need. Every time you go off in search of one of these items, you'll break your flow. Break it too often and it will disappear.

→ **Consider the conditions.** The space in which we rehearse, and the time we write, are so vital that the next chapter is all about them.

→ **Get quick feedback.** Ask and react. Tennis coaches speak to a player during a match to change their hand grip or court position. Immediate feedback stimulates flow.

→ **Please be kind to yourself.** Storytelling nirvana isn't reached every day. Some days are just harder than others. Even the best storytellers in the world have off-days. *All's Well that Ends Well* is a tough watch, *Die Another Day* is a duff Bond movie, and many Jane Austen fans don't like *Mansfield Park*.

## Flow at work

**You are responsible for your flow. No matter what's thrown at you, you can change your conditions and approach to make writing easier and more fun.**

→ **If a task seems too difficult ...**

→ **Chunk it down.** Writing a book of 40,000 words becomes easier when you see it as 20 chapters. A chapter becomes less daunting when you split it into 6 sections, and each section becomes a breeze when you see it as 6 or 7 paragraphs. You'll never write a book in one sitting, but you can produce the first draft of a paragraph in 10 minutes once you've got your flow.

→ **Ask for help** from the person who's commissioned the writing. It could be that the brief isn't clear, or you haven't understood their needs. Most clients (internal or external) are eager to save time and will point you in the right direction. It's in their interest to help you with objectives.

→ **Guerrilla writing.** This is especially beneficial with bigger projects. In the days before the official start date jot down ideas, write a couple of lines, doodle a mind map or two. You might not use any of this preparatory work, but your mind will be receptive to flow when you kick off for real.

→ **If a task seems too easy ...**

→ **Ask for more.** Again, personal responsibility is key. You have to ask for more testing work or your development will grind to a halt. We all need to feel that we're moving to the right on the degree of challenge axis.

→ **Become a mentor.** You can also 'diversify yourself' and be a coach for other writers on the team. You've got the skills, and now it's time to pass them on.

→ **Invest in your soft skills.** Learning how to manage people and give feedback may boost your career. If you're primarily a writer, think about improving your performance skills. If you're mostly a stand-up storyteller, take a course in creative writing. If you work as a journalist, why not learn how to manage a team?

# Where to Next?

→  To follow up these themes, look at:

- Chapter 3: If you can't find your story-writing flow, go back to our four micro-story structures. Set up the two-step boxes, write key words and wait for inspiration to strike when you're in the shower and don't have a pen.

- Chapter 13: This chapter about finding the ideal conditions for writing will make a big difference to your flow.

- Chapter 15: Feedback is a really important part of the flow process, so learn how to dish it out and take it.

→  Look for this. Can you see someone who's got their flow on? Good places to look include the gym, stand-up comedy shows, music gigs and even libraries.

# Creating your ideal conditions

The right time and the right place boost the quantity and quality of your writing. Blocks and barriers evaporate when you establish your routine.

# Writer's Block does and doesn't exist

**Have you ever suffered from Accountant's Block? When the creativity you need to save your spreadsheet is lacking and your balance sheet has lost its flow?**

Of course not. We all know Accountant's Block is a figment of the imagination. We accept that the accountant is tired or bored or fed up with office life, but we don't ascribe his lack of productivity to a lack of inspiration. We tell him to take a break, have a coffee, stretch his legs or hit the gym. We're sure he'll come back raring to have another go at the income statement.

Our approach to creative blocks betrays a very different attitude. I bet we've all suffered – and darling, I mean really *suffered* – from Writer's Block. Yes, I see you nodding sadly in agreement. It's flared up again, and there's even some secondary procrastination in the diagnosis. You slump over your desk, head in hands, and moan that there's nothing you can do about it.

I beg to differ.

# The three Rs of writing

**Writer's Block is actually an essential part of the writing process. Rebrand it as 'thinking time' and it immediately feels like a gift rather than a problem.**

There are many ways to get your brain ready to write. Here's a selection of techniques that always work for me.

→ **Ritual tells your brain it's time to create.** Your brain associates an object or action with an activity. Depending on your age, you play 'You Should Be Dancing', 'Dancing on my Own' or 'Dancing with our Hands Tied' before you go out on a Saturday night. You rub your palms together when you approach the pull-up bars in the park. It doesn't matter if these cognitive cues are deliberate or completely unself-conscious. They tell you it's time to begin.

What ritual can you employ? For me, placing my pen and notebook on the right-hand side of my desk always works, even though I do most of my writing on my laptop.

It's illogical and a little silly, but I'm not going to change my routine, because it works every time.

→ **Routine shows you're committed to write.** Every successful writer has a routine. They're at their desk at 6am and stop when the kids wake up, or they wait till midnight strikes before they write a single word. J.K. Rowling went to the same café every day to write *Harry Potter*; Maya Angelou did crosswords and played solitaire while her 'Big Mind' delved into mysteries.

Lucky pencils and your magic cardigan play a part in routine, but the most important aspect is – quite simply – to keep writing. Never waste your time waiting for the ideal external conditions to arrive. They probably won't.

Here are three quick tips to establish your routine:

*Set yourself achievable targets.* Commit to five hundred words before you can get a coffee. Keep your motivation strong by chunking down big writing tasks into doable sections.

*It's a job, so clock in.* Treat your flow space as your writing factory. This isn't where you daydream, doubt your talent or bitch on Twitter about constant interruptions. No. This is where you write.

*Twenty minutes at a time.* Set your alarm and then ignore all interruptions. Twenty minutes of hard, focused writing is always worth more than a morning of aimless dithering.

→ **Regularity gives you writing muscles.**

You may not write every day at work, so suddenly being asked to write a speech by lunchtime or draft the chairman's statement for your firm's annual report is a big ask. It's like running a 10k six months after you last went for a jog. It's no wonder you feel stress.

Keep your writing muscles strong and flexible with regular micro-tasks. We can all find one writing 'exercise' every day to keep the blood flowing. It could be stripping down a wordy marketing pitch or making your LinkedIn profile sound human. Take every opportunity to practise. Volunteer to take on any writing tasks that are available.

*'I have met so many people who say they've got a book in them, but they've never written a word. To be a writer – this may seem trite, I realize – you have to actually write. You have to write every day, and you have to write whether you feel like it or not.'*
*Khaled Hosseini*

## Where and when do writers write?

**Biographies of writers always contain a chapter on their writing habit. It's as if we only need to wear Emily Dickinson's glasses or sit at Charles Dickens's desk to become a success. Fans become obsessed with their favourite authors' routines, be it Toni Morrison's need to write before dawn broke or W.H. Auden's breakfasting on nothing more than Benzedrine.**

The combination of a blank screen and a tight deadline can be so terrifying that we freeze. But all you need to create the ideal conditions is to ask yourself: am I a Monk or am I a Rock Star?

In the film *The Dirt* (2018), the future Mötley Crüe drummer Tommy Lee first meets the songwriter Nikki Sixx in an all-night diner. The place is noisy and it's past midnight, but Nikki doesn't seem too bothered when a nervous Tommy (dressed in his sister's leopard-skin trousers) approaches him. Why not? Nikki is a night owl who loves to write when the sun is down. He thrives on the energy of an adoring audience, so he likes a buzzy place that will keep him stimulated.

Scroll back to fourteenth-century Italy and the eerie silence of a Benedictine abbey. In Umberto Eco's novel *The Name of the Rose* (1980; filmed in 1986), the monks in the library work in absolute silence. It's not just the darkness that makes them prefer working in the early morning; getting up early to illustrate manuscripts at their oak desks is an act of devotion. There must be absolutely no interruptions. Shhh!

Both Nikki and the monk have found their perfect writing environment. And you can do the same by considering the three most important factors: Time, Space and Noise.

→ **Time.** The best time for you to write is determined by your body clock. Are you like the monk, who dips his quill into the ink just as dawn breaks through the cloister windows? Or does inspiration strike you when the moon is high?

Don't fight your body clock. Also, absolutely no one writes well in the two hours after lunch. A full tummy is the enemy of good writing. Believe me, I've done the research.

→ **Space.** Entering the right physical space is a very strong cognitive cue for you to write. As soon as you close the door behind you or jam on your headphones, you're telling your mind to write.

Carving out a space that you control is vital. The monk sits at the same desk he's had for thirty years, and hates interruptions when he's in flow. Writing is a solo activity.

Other business writers need people around them to perform. Like the rock star, they're nothing without an audience. Sometimes it's all about the peer pressure. You don't want to be seen doing nothing in front of your friends, so you work hard and push through any blocks. And sometimes a packed office or coffee shop gives us the energy we need to complete our tasks.

Writing at home is something I love, but it took time for me to perfect my routine. I start writing within fifteen minutes of waking. I can do more in the next ninety minutes at home than in a whole day in an office. The early mornings I spent on packed Tube trains wasted my most creative moments. Now that so many of us are working at home, you might be able to take control of your schedule to block out time for creativity.

I'm very conscious of marking out my space. I make sure the desk is clear of anything not work-related. Dirty plates, my daughter's homework and novels are all tidied up the night before. If I'm working on a big report, printouts and mind maps cover the floor.

→ **Noise.** Here's where people are very different. Complete silence can put even the most conscientious monk on edge. White noise or whale music can reduce the impact of sudden sounds at home. In the office, headphones send out a strong do-not-disturb vibe that marks out your territory.

The Netflix version of Mötley Crüe and the Sean Connery version of *The Name of the Rose*.

Other people love the camaraderie of a packed trading floor or a busy studio. Short chats recharge their batteries, but silence sends them to sleep. I always have music on at home, but it has to be something I already know. Halfway through a lengthy client brief isn't the best time for the latest banger from Skrillex. Every distraction other than music ruins my concentration. So, I disconnect from the internet and switch off all my phones. Try it for an hour. Your productivity will rocket.

There's nothing rigorously scientific in my advice. I've found my ideal working environment through trial and error, and luck. The next step is for you to find your own. Writing is a very personal skill, so it's worth investing time finding out where you sit on the monk–rock star spectrum. Like 99 per cent of the working world, you'll be a mixture. Unless, of course, you're already working as either a monk or a rock star, in which case you're probably not that bothered about writing your next exec summary anyway.

Let the rule be 'each to their own'.

# A little job for you

**If you've got this far into the book you're obviously someone who wants to write more. Take some time now to define your ideal working conditions. You need to know what's good for you so that you can avoid environments that make you tense, annoyed, frustrated or even angry.**

Here's what you need to do. Think about how time, space and noise affect you. Jot down what works and what doesn't. This may well be the most revealing six minutes of your day.

|         | What works | What doesn't |
|---------|------------|--------------|
| Time    |            |              |
| Space   |            |              |
| Noise   |            |              |

# The joy of the blank page

**Grab a sheet of A4 paper. You're going to fill it with writing in less than ten minutes.**

Start the clock!

→ **Write down** three things you can see but are too far away to touch. It could be your favourite mug, which you can't reach without getting up from your chair; it could be the sky.

→ **Write down** three things that you love but cannot currently see, anything from an abstract emotion (universal peace) to a favourite food (Nutella).

→ **Imagine** you are in the time zone that's exactly twelve hours ahead of you. Write down three things you'd see right now.

→ **Write down** five of the adjectives you want your voice to represent. Flip back to Chapter 11 if you need a reminder.

→ **Write out** this sentence: 'I am a happy person who wants happiness.'

→ **Write out** the sentence again but change 'happy' to one of your adjectives.

→ **Change** 'happiness' to one of the things that are too far away to touch, cannot be seen or are in the different time zone.

→ **Keep going**, changing the verb and even the narrator as you fill the page.

What just happened? You exchanged a blank page for a full one. You mind is open and much more receptive to new ideas. You know you have a technique to smash through writer's block if it ever appears again. Your pen or pencil is magically connected to the page. You know that writing is easy ...

## Where to Next?

→ To follow up these themes, look at:

- Chapter 3: Sometimes stories elude us because we're unsure of their impact on others. Review Cialdini's principles and see if you can tie one into your tale.

- Chapter 5: Are there any barriers between you and your story that you can remove?

- Chapter 8: Review the ways we can all turn on our creativity, whatever the time of day or the space in which we find ourselves.

→ **Dream First Class.** If you had complete freedom to be creative, where would you work? What would your space look like, and what country would it be in? Let your mind wander until you visualize exactly what you want.

# CHAPTER 14

# Ways to improve your writing style

Word choice counts. You have a duty of care towards the audience sitting expectantly in front of you. You have to be hyper-conscious of your language to get them – and keep them – on your side.

# Word choice attracts and repels

**How to make this introductory paragraph as dull as humanly possible? I could make this sentence super-long and fill it with embedded subclauses, resulting in lots of commas and even the old semi-colon; the best way to lose readers and negatively influence listeners is to deliberately pick long words, obscure jargon terms and the appalling clichés of bizspeak like 'core values', 'proactive synergies' and 'granular empowerment strategy'.**

Easy, no? I've turned you against me, my story and my ideas in a matter of seconds.

There are two parts to improving your choice of words. First, you have to avoid the word traps[1] that are hidden all around our places of work. Second, you have to actively choose a vocabulary that attracts listeners, watchers and readers.

*The secret of being boring is to say everything.*
Voltaire

# How to avoid the four biggest word traps

**Remember your audience at all times. Keep jargon and bizspeak to a minimum.**

→ **Keep jargon in its place.**

I'm not going to say that all jargon is bad. It develops naturally within groups as a way of speeding up communication. For example, acronyms such as SME have a really clear meaning for their users. When you are talking to a room full of industry experts, there's no need to explain technical terms that they already know.

Sometimes jargon is so good that the whole world uses it. We 'Google' someone rather than 'looking them up on the internet'. No one has ever 'Binged' someone, have they?

---

1    'Word trap' is a phrase I've just made up to sound different and original. You may not like it, but it's made you pay attention. If you're reading this footnote, my risk has paid off.

But the danger occurs when jargon jumps into the wider world without being fully understood. Is SME short for 'Subject Matter Expert' or 'Small or Medium-sized Enterprise'? If you have to use jargon when talking to non-experts, please 'translate' it the first time it appears, or certain members of your audience will feel excluded.

### → Cut down on the business-speak, going forward.

The boring robot-speak used in Bizlandia should be chopped out of every story. These ugly words and clichés are the super-strength Mogadon of presentations, able to send your audience into deep sleep within minutes. People tune out when they hear this language, and will judge you as someone lacking in original thought. There's nothing that shows your lack of innovation better than using the word 'innovation' in every second sentence.

### → Be a Latin translator.

The English language is a great borrower of words. Do you know that 'daughter' is derived from Sanskrit or that 'anorak' was originally a word in Eskimo-Aleut? I thought not.

One advantage this gives English is that there are normally two different ways to say the same thing. The first one – more formal, slightly courtly – originated in Latin. The Latin words usually have three or four syllables and so take up more space on the page.

When speaking naturally, however, we tend to pick short words – get, hold, hit – which have Anglo-Saxon or Norse roots. Choosing these words will speed up your delivery and make you sound less like a lecturer and more like a friend.

### → Choose short words over long words.

There's a certain vocabulary that people use when they don't know what they're talking about. They'll use long-winded phrases – 'at this present moment in time' for 'now' – instead of getting to the point.

These ready-made phrases give the speaker time to think while words are coming out of their mouth. They may also

| Your Latin tutor says | A storyteller says |
| --- | --- |
| Terminate | End |
| Request | Ask |
| Demonstrate | Show |
| Prohibit | Ban |
| Inform | Tell |
| Administer | Give |
| Elevate | Lift |
| Transform | Change |

| A pompous politician says | A storyteller says |
| --- | --- |
| Magnitude | Size |
| Purchase | Buy |
| Due to the fact that | Because |
| In the event that | If |
| In advance of | Before |
| For the purpose of | For |
| With the exception of | Except |
| In connection with | About |

give the speaker a false sense of confidence, making him or her misguidedly believe that, *ceteris paribus*, the odd Latin or French phrase makes them appear intrinsically superior.

Watch out for a move towards the pompous. It's often a clue that the speaker is struggling with the topic. As a storyteller, go for the shorter alternative every time.

## The Roulette Wheel

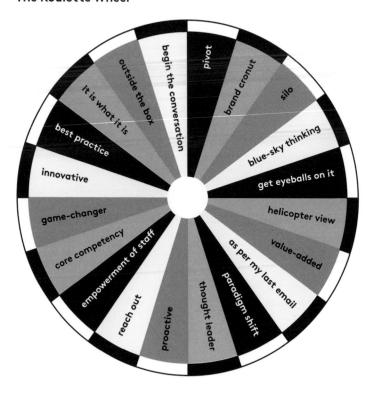

pivot · brand cronut · silo · blue-sky thinking · get eyeballs on it · helicopter view · value-added · as per my last email · paradigm shift · thought leader · proactive · reach out · empowerment of staff · core competency · game-changer · innovative · best practice · It is what it is · outside the box · begin the conversation

● Dated clichés          ○ Hated words and phrases

● Clumsy and overused     ● No one understands these

We all detest these worn-out words and phrases, yet their use is on the rise. Is there someone you know who's guilty of these irritating clichés? Instead of breaking their fingers, show them this wheel as a gentle reminder that other words are available.

# Use the vocabulary of storytelling

**Up to now, this chapter has been about words to avoid. Now, in a sudden twist, I want to concentrate on the words you should choose when you're telling stories.**

### → Anchor your story in time.

There are good reasons why fairy stories begin with 'Once upon a time'. The Brothers Grimm are telling their readers to switch on the story-listening part of their brains. The story is placed firmly in the past and has a clear, unambiguous starting point. When someone in the audience retells your story, this is where they'll begin.

Instead of being vague, with phrases such as 'back in the day' or 'in the past', make a conscious effort to anchor your story. Avoid calendar dates ('it was 13 February 2021') in favour of descriptions that have a greater emotional connection ('it was the eve of St Valentine's Day').

Tying your date to an event or person creates a stronger sense of time in the listener's mind. Phrases like 'it was the week that Dr Ograbek started as head of infection control' or 'two days before the January sales ground to a halt' create a 'timestamp' visual.

### → Make the sequence of events clear.

We underestimate the work done by simple sequence words when telling a story. Understanding is always improved when we use 'firstly', 'then', 'next' and 'finally'. Phrases such as 'beginning with', 'when it's ready' and 'at this stage' walk a listener through a complicated process. And make sure you end with a definite marker. It's probably best to avoid 'they all lived happily ever after', but there's nothing wrong with 'when the first stage was complete', or 'they were now ready to launch'.

A popular construction with storytellers is an ongoing action in the past that is interrupted by another event. For example, 'Miss Pavalkyte was transferring the money when Mrs Fabiano called.' You're showing a logical connection between events, and there's that sudden change of direction which is always good for storytelling.

### → Listeners like the logic of cause and effect.

By the time you tell your story, you should know it inside out. The temptation then is to speed up and drop the connectors that link sentences and paragraphs. Don't! These words and phrases take up very little space, yet they weave together the different story elements by explaining causation and motivation.

Take your listeners by the hand and guide them through your story with simple words like 'because' and 'since'. An effect caused by an event in the past can be introduced with 'as a consequence of their research' or 'owing to the findings in Professor Henderson's report'. A future event that occurs because of a current event can be introduced with 'causing', 'leading to' or 'resulting in'.

### → Make it clear when you change the point of view.

Introducing a character who disagrees with you is a good way to show you're open to the opinions of others. Phrases such as 'looking at the problem from Yvonne Leckie's perspective' or 'if I were in Emmanuel's shoes' make it clear that you're presenting a different angle.

Some of these phrases can be used sneakily. If you want to show that you don't have a high opinion of the alternative view, use 'others believed' or 'some people thought'. And whenever you say 'let me play devil's advocate for a moment', you're hinting that your opposition is largely theoretical.

### → Guide your readers when you introduce additional information.

Link words work well in stories and more traditional presentations. If you're adding more details, slip in 'moreover' and the more casual 'also' and 'as well as'. Examples that back up your findings can be introduced with 'similarly'; examples that support an alternative hypothesis can follow 'in contrast'.

Variations on 'This is a good place to mention/introduce/ talk about ...' have saved my hide when I couldn't find the right linking word.

### → Highlight twists and surprises.

They are not to be overused, but 'suddenly' and 'all of a sudden' do have their place in storytelling. You can also hint at subterfuge and skulduggery with 'without telling us' and 'what Joseph kept secret was ...'

My personal favourite is 'unbeknownst to me'. I know it's old-fashioned and self-consciously literary, but every time I hear it, I visualize a detective in an Agatha Christie novel who is about to reveal the murderer. You have my permission to use it.

## Where to Next?

→ To follow up these themes, look at:

- Chapter 5: Will you change your thoughts on barriers to communication, now that you know more about the importance of word choice?

- Chapter 9: Go back to the story you sketched out on overcoming an obstacle. I told you at the time, 'Don't worry about being perfect, just get the words down on the page.' Now is a good time to ignore those instructions and write it properly.

- Chapter 16: Choosing short words over long is a good way to boost your ethos in front of an audience.

→ Watch for this. Look for moments when a speaker turns pompous. This often occurs when they're forced 'off-script' by an unexpected challenge.

# CHAPTER 15

# Polish that diamond

Feedback is tricky. You've got to categorize it before you can use it well – and you must recognize the emotions at play when you invite others to critique your work.

# Don't rush the final check just because you're pushed for time

**Congratulations, you're almost there. But, before you press 'send' or upload the video, hold on.**

We're all keen to cross a big item off the To Do list, but what you've got in front of you is still just an early version of what you want to achieve. Five per cent extra effort now will double the quality of your output.

The two stages we need to consider are **feedback** and **proofing**. Years ago, if you were working as a journalist or report-writer, a subeditor would do all that for you. Now it's likely that you will do your own checking and proofing. Depending on where you work, getting feedback may be a struggle.

I normally mark this transition from being a writer to being an editor with a walk along the beach or a break for food and drink. This pause helps me change my mindset. I refocus on the reader or listener and remind myself of my intended FAB.

## All feedback isn't created equal

**I split feedback into four types. I'll give you an example of each and tell you how to use it.**

### → Complimentary feedback

<u>Looks like:</u> 'This is awesome, don't change a single comma.'
<u>What's good about it:</u> You feel super-confident and start preparing your acceptance speech for the Nobel Prize in Literature.
<u>The danger:</u> Everything can be improved, so it's likely that they haven't bothered to read it. It may also be that they are in love with you or are too scared to tell you what they really think.

### → Suggestive feedback

<u>Looks like:</u> 'This is good enough to send out to clients, but next time let's talk about structure and use of headlines.'

<u>What's good about it:</u> Phew! You can send it out without more work.

<u>Act on this:</u> Their ideas will lead to you improving over the long term. Make sure you find time to talk to them and listen to their ideas. Perhaps they'll even be open to mentoring you.

### → Advisory feedback

<u>Looks like:</u> 'Don't send this out yet. We need to change the structure and use of headlines.'

<u>What's good about it:</u> Close, but it's not ready. There are changes you need to make now.

<u>Stamp your feet, then act on it:</u> This will probably mean a late night, but you can benefit from immediate learning.

### → Destructive feedback

<u>Looks like:</u> 'I hate all of this. Change everything!'

<u>What's good about it:</u> It is now 100 per cent clear to you that the person reviewing your work is an idiot. They hate you, but only because – deep down in the dark recesses of their soul – they hate themselves.

<u>Ignore them, but in a strategic way:</u> It doesn't matter if they are having a bad day or a bad life, there's no excuse for this aggression. My advice in the short term is to make their changes, but only once they've explained the *why* and the *what* in much more detail. Longer term, it's about finding a different person to give you feedback and/or putting a dead fish in their desk drawer the day they go on holiday.

# Blessed are those who give feedback

**Most of us are uncomfortable giving feedback to friends and colleagues.**

We don't know how to express our comments without hurting their feelings. We may feel underqualified and lacking in writing skills ourselves. We don't want to display our lack of knowledge on the subject and we certainly don't want to rock the boat by giving negative feedback to someone above us in the hierarchy.

So give thanks to anyone who offers you high-quality feedback. Then do the right thing, and return the favour. One technique I often recommend is to find a feedback buddy, someone you can swap work with regularly.

You don't have to agree with every item of feedback you get, because sometimes your original writing will be better than the suggestions you're given. But you still have to give thanks to those who have taken the time and effort to critique your work. Act like a know-it-all big shot and you'll soon find helpers thin on the ground.

# Let's be honest – feedback can be painful

**I always get an emotional response to feedback. Even though I've written articles, essays, reports, novels and non-fiction books, I still feel nervous about opening an email from my editor.**

However I dress it up, they're basically correcting my mistakes, so it's going to be a recap of all I've done wrong and everything they don't like. No one, if they are honest, would admit to looking forward to that.

It's important to be aware of your emotional reaction to feedback. We all have a bad memory of an essay covered in red ink or a report thrown in the bin, but negative feelings such as anger, fear and frustration can get in the way of success. If you notice tension or irritation when someone comments on your work, stop and think about the three Ps of feedback:

→ **Keep things in perspective.**

Everything is fixable; nothing is inscribed in granite. Often people will recommend minor changes while accepting 99 per cent of your submission. It's changing the colour of the bathroom, not knocking down the whole house.

→ **Feedback is not personal.**

Remind yourself that feedback is given on your work, not your worth. People aren't passing judgement on you as a person.

## → **Stay positive.**

These people are your helpers, not your enemies. They're stopping you from making silly errors in public, and for that we should all be grateful.

I get hit by negative thoughts every time I receive feedback. My own personal feedback loop mixes high efficiency with moments of dark despair. I'll share it with you. It splits into two distinct parts: the **downside** and the **upside** (see opposite). My emotions and actions follow exactly the same pattern, whether it's feedback on a highly numerical report or on a storytelling session about the productivity hacks of prolific crime novelists.

The Downside begins with a skim through the comments I've received from my editor. I want to gauge *how much* needs changing and *how deep* the changes need to be. Does it need a few commas, or does it need a totally different chapter? I take note of my emotional response – am I happy or sad about the feedback? My mental state will affect how I approach my edits.

Now, because I know just how much effort it is to give feedback, I thank the sender for their ideas and support *before* I make the changes. Then I dive in. The first thing I do is go for some **quick wins**. This is when I correct grammar and punctuation errors, silly spelling mistakes and sloppily constructed sentences. It's easy to make rapid improvements in this way, and that always feels positive.

I'm now ready for the Upside. My report or presentation has already improved, so I face the heavy lifting of changing structure and even writing new sections with confidence. I accept that maybe I need to kill some darlings by getting rid of wordy explanations and irrelevant material. This is tough work, so I make sure I take regular breaks. It's normally now that I start to feel much better about my work (and, as a consequence, about myself).

When I've finished, I always check my changes with care. It's too easy at this stage to make silly mistakes because I'm either frustrated to still be working on it or giddy with the excitement of nearly finishing. And then I get ready for proofing.

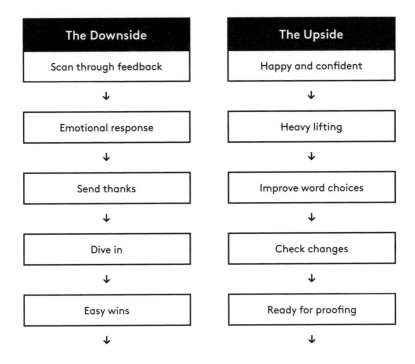

| The Downside | The Upside |
|---|---|
| Scan through feedback | Happy and confident |
| ↓ | ↓ |
| Emotional response | Heavy lifting |
| ↓ | ↓ |
| Send thanks | Improve word choices |
| ↓ | ↓ |
| Dive in | Check changes |
| ↓ | ↓ |
| Easy wins | Ready for proofing |
| ↓ | ↓ |

## Proofing is another mindset

**Proofing – also known as 'proofreading' or (joke alert) 'profing' – is the final check of that LinkedIn article before you post it online. We do it to spot annoying errors and also to check the overall consistency of the project. Proofing takes place *after* feedback and editing.**

Proofing appeals to the completer-finisher gene in me, but I know it's a pain in the neck for most people. Everyone will take a different approach, but I've got eight tips for you:

1. **Keep a Before copy.** Send this to yourself or save it to the cloud. It'll protect you from any fatal screw-ups during proofing.
2. **Print and hide.** Print out everything you've done so far, then hide it until tomorrow morning. You need fresh eyes for this final stage of checking.

3. **Focus on names.** People love seeing their names in print, so make sure you get them right. I know my surname is rare, but you should know how to use Ctrl/C and Ctrl/V by now. The same applies to the names of products, companies and places.
4. **Be careful with numbers.** Is that billions of dollars or millions of yen? Is the decimal point in the correct place throughout the document? Stick the wrong number up in your first slide and your credibility is blown before you've even opened your mouth.
5. **Check the structural markers.** Make sure headlines and titles tell the story on their own. If you've changed the text below, make sure the header is still relevant.
6. **Look for error clusters.** Mistakes gang up in areas where we didn't know the subject very well or when we were tired. If you find two mistakes close to each other, I bet you'll find a third and a fourth nearby.
7. **Read aloud.** Absolutely essential for speeches, of course, but worth considering for written documents as well. This is also the best way to get commas in the right place – you need a punctuation mark every time you pause for breath. (Reading aloud looks a bit odd in offices, but it's not a problem for home workers.)
8. **Run spellcheck.** It's not as perfect a tool as Microsoft would have us believe, but it's an essential step. Use the grammar settings properly and it'll catch annoying errors such as *they're/their/there* and *two/too/to*.

# Where to Next?

→ To follow up these themes, look at:

- Chapter 2: A key part of my revision routine is to remind myself of my original FAB, to confirm that I've covered my objectives convincingly.

- Chapter 11: When you review the work of others, be conscious of words and sentences that don't fit the author's voice.

→ <u>Think about this.</u> We've focused a lot on written presentations, so now watch some speeches. Avoid the classics (Mandela on unity, Malala on education) because they'll only make you feel small. Instead, look for people who don't make speeches often. Watch for the difference between a rehearser and a bluffer. It may not be clear to the speaker, but it's always crystal-clear to a viewer.

# PART 4

# Wha
# Learn
# the M

t We

from

asters

# CHAPTER 16

# Ethos, pathos and logos

Follow the advice of a master: to be a wonderful orator you must demonstrate your ability as a speaker, your emotional impact on the audience and your skill in using evidence.

# Aristotle cracked the art of presentation in about 345 BCE

**How's this for an impressive CV? This man was taught by Plato and became Alexander the Great's personal tutor. He was an ancient Greek who founded the Lyceum of Athens, an expert in everything from aesthetics to zoology, an influence on every aspect of Western knowledge to this day.**

Meet Aristotle, whose name means 'the best purpose'.

Aristotle wrote non-stop, but his papyrus scrolls have not survived the ravages of time. All we have are notes made by his diligent students. (He was that rare specimen, a writer whose first drafts were good enough to be published.) The fact that we're still talking about his 'modes of persuasion' some 2,400 years after he first came up with them suggests he's a man to follow.

Most books on presentation skills focus on the absolute basics: make sure people can see the screen, don't fold your arms across your chest, try not to be boring. But successful presentations are about much more than moving slickly between slides. Aristotle identified three elements that make a successful presentation. His 'triad' can be (very) summarized as:

Ethos: the speaker
Pathos: the audience
Logos: the logic of the speech

As we add detail to these three words, you'll see that they are the basis of how we judge every communication. This three-element approach is as applicable to non-fiction books as it is to political speeches, brand identities and corporate calls to action. But I'm going to focus on live, stand-up storytelling.

I'm a big fan of Aristotle, as you can probably tell. So much so that I'm going to sprinkle some of his best pieces of advice throughout this chapter.

*Education is bitter, but its fruit is sweet.*

What better motivation can there be to continue with this chapter?

# Ethos occurs once you've established your personal credibility

**Before listening to any presenter, we ask ourselves 'What gives them the right to talk to us about this?' The answers we seek reflect the principles of influence we covered in Chapter 3.**

→ **The audience looks for credentials and experience.** That's why our 'war medals' are so vital. The audience wants to know that you struggled with doubt, overcame problems, defeated enemies and went through the arc of change that all good heroes experience.

This isn't the place for meaningless job titles, nor the time for fake humility. The audience wants people who have achieved greatness, and you need to tell them what you've done. Real status comes from our success as subject experts, business leaders or recognized authorities, or by being good human beings.

→ **Knowledge and connection keep people listening.** You don't have to be the cleverest person in the room, but you have to be the absolute expert in the topic. Now's the time to mention your master's degree in the subject and that internship at a competitor last year. If everyone listening is an industry insider, use the right jargon without explanation or apology. Showing you are similar to your audience is a great way to establish ethos.

We've all heard politicians waffle about subjects they don't understand. Not only do we reject the speech they're currently stumbling through, but we will always regard them with scepticism in the future. Lying, poor preparation and being out of date destroy your ethos.

**Speaker's character**

Comes from
• Expertise
• Status
• Learning

ETHOS

THE MESSAGE

→ **How to appeal with ethos.**

Ethos is both intrinsic and growable. Part of it is inherent – instinct tells us if a person has integrity and is worthy of our respect. But there are ways you can demonstrate that you're a person of value. Take courses, read widely, spend time with genuine people who share good ideas. Increase your credibility to get more listeners.

*We are what we do repeatedly.*
*Excellence, then, is a habit, not an action.*

Shame on you if you thought this was coined by Oprah Winfrey or Deepak Chopra! It's Aristotle's explanation of how everyone can build up their ethos over time

## Pathos connects you emotionally to your audience

Successful presentations change how we feel. Ten minutes ago we were unconnected, uninterested, uninvolved. Now we are angry, sad, inspired, frustrated, happy, ready to surrender or eager to fight. We've all used the phrase 'a moving speech', but how many of us have ever considered what it took to move us?

Pathos – the root of words such as 'empathy' and 'pathetic' – occurs when our audience feels exactly what we want them to feel.

→ **Storytelling skills create pathos.** *The Silence of the Lambs* is one of only three films to have won the big five Oscars (best Picture, Director, Actor, Actress and Screenplay). The director, Jonathan Demme, has complete dominion over the viewer; he makes us tremble with fear, or laugh with relief, or close our eyes in pain *exactly* when he wants. The emotional bond he creates between us and the hero, Clarice Starling, means that we are afraid when she's at risk and joyful when she kills the baddie. Demme is such a skilled storyteller that we even share the emotions of the film's ostensible villain, Hannibal Lecter.

→ **Great storytelling provokes emotions that connect your audience to you.** Pathos comes from a punchy retelling of your 'war stories', those tales of courage in the face of adversity or of flashes of inspiration, that out-of-this-world solution to an age-old problem or that Zoom meeting that changed your life.

Pathos is about them, not about you. A speaker with tons of personal credibility (ethos) may be the best person for the job, but unless they can connect with the audience it's a waste of time.

People who are forever appealing to our emotions leave us exhausted. (This applies to life in general, not just to storytelling and speech-making!) If the emotional appeal isn't supported by the speaker's character (ethos) and the

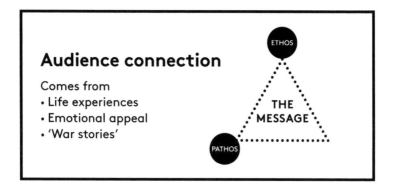

**Audience connection**

Comes from
• Life experiences
• Emotional appeal
• 'War stories'

ETHOS

THE MESSAGE

PATHOS

quality of the speech (logos), we're going to be left feeling manipulated. Use pathos sparingly, otherwise you'll be the over-emotional speaker who makes everyone else feel awkward.

→ **Boost pathos through word choice.** The simplest thing to do is change your vocabulary so the audience feels you are on the same side. There's an amazing example of this in Albert Camus's classic *The Plague* (1947). In the first sermon delivered by the priest Paneloux, he addresses his congregation as 'you', as if he's above and apart from them. By the time of his second sermon, Paneloux has acknowledged the destructive power of the plague and is beginning to doubt God's desire to save his flock. He now uses the pronoun 'we'. He's no longer an observer on the sidelines, but a participant in the struggle. He connects with his flock through their shared suffering and pain.

→ **Body language helps you connect.** Make eye contact with your listeners to keep them energized. Use open arms to suggest that you're open-minded. Nod your head and focus your attention when you are asked a question. And mimic the emotions you want to provoke with your body: laugh to convey happiness, tighten your fists in frustration or shake them to show you're ready for a fight.

I've noticed that many speakers display tense, inflexible body language on Zoom, Skype and FaceTime. Make sure that you can't see yourself as you're talking; there's nothing less likely to create natural body language than seeing your every nod and grimace. Your colleagues will focus on your head and neck, so any gestures – a wave of the hand for 'maybe', steepled fingers to suggest reflection – must be above the collar line.

*A speaker who is attempting to move people to thought or action must concern himself with Pathos.*

Aristotle knew that the speaker's credentials or the contents of his speech aren't enough on their own to make an impact.

# Logos is about knowing when and how to use your facts

*Logos* **is ancient Greek for 'word', and it's the root of 'logic'.**[1] **If pathos was all about the emotions, logos is concerned with reason. It considers factors such as evidence, statistics, structure and learning we've gleaned from the past.**

Economists employ logos all the time. Everyone arguing for an increase in government spending after Covid-19 uses statistics such as 'GDP is down 15 per cent' and 'Unemployment is up 20 per cent.' They'll reach a conclusion based on past evidence that appears to be a logical outcome of these figures: 'We need $200 billion to get the economy back on track.'

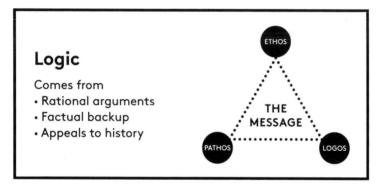

## Logic

Comes from
- Rational arguments
- Factual backup
- Appeals to history

→ **Make your structure so clear it can disappear.** Take your listener on a journey. You need to be clear about their starting point: what do they currently know about the topic, and what do they want to learn from you? Each step on the way must connect with its predecessor. And when you arrive at the end, they must feel that no other destination was logical. If your structure is strong yet invisible the audience will feel that they've actually got to your conclusion before you. They'll feel intellectually empowered, and that's a great way to get them on your side.

---

1    Without wishing to sound like my dad, the Greek word *logos* translates as 'I say'. Over the years it's come to mean opinion, speech, reason and discourse, among many other things.

Hands up if you think Victor Kiam is showing off an early version of the iPhone.

→ **<u>Use facts and stats to convince.</u>** Your audience will be swayed by evidence. What's the graphic that will change their mind, what's the trend that will stop them in their tracks?

Now's the time to be specific. No one wants vague abstractions when you're talking about mortality rates.

We also benefit from **citing authorities**: talking about the experts who back up our claims and using quotations to support and illustrate. An oldie but a goldie is Victor Kiam talking about Remington shavers: 'I liked the shaver so much, I bought the company.'

*All knowledge should be subject to examination and reason.*

Aristotle knew that ethos and pathos create reactions, but that without the backup of logos their power will fade.

Some closing thoughts on Aristotelian rhetoric. The boundaries between ethos, pathos and logos are more blurry than many people realize. The terms overlap and their meanings have changed over the millennia, so we can be forgiven for using them with less precision than Aristotle's students would have done. And – most importantly – while good speakers may use one of these characteristics, the great speakers will display all three.

## Where to Next?

To follow up these themes, look at:

> Chapter 3: Focusing on the audience is very much about pathos.

> Chapter 7: Classic story structures are a balance between pathos and logos.

> Chapter 18: Data-driven storytelling is where logos and pathos combine.

→ Think about this. I've used ethos, pathos and logos throughout this chapter.

Ethos: You must believe in my ability to write about this topic before you 'believe' this chapter. To persuade you I've shown a breadth of learning (Aristotle, Camus) balanced with references from popular culture (*Silence of the Lambs*, Oprah, Deepak).

Pathos: I've been specific with pronouns and possessives. I've used 'we' 21 times, 'us' 7 times and 'our' 6 times, and even sneaked in 'ourselves' once.

Logos: I've cited Aristotle from the first line. My examples show that his ideas have not only stood the test of time, but are flourishing.

What other examples can you find?

# CHAPTER 17

# Reading for fun and for profit

Every great writer is an avid reader.
We can all learn a huge amount about
motivation and conflict from novels,
scripts and non-fiction.

# The rise of the billionaire bibliophile

**Reading books is cool again. We're bored with video games and sick of social media. Many YouTube influencers have stopped talking about their favourite eyeliner or the optimum number of pull-up reps, to share what books are influencing them.**

The focus is on learning, self-improvement and generating new ideas. Elon Musk speaks of reading two books a day when he was younger, but they were engineering textbooks. Warren Buffett spends 80 per cent of his office time reading, but it's mostly corporate reports and his five daily newspapers. It's only in recent years that Bill Gates, a book-a-week man, has added novels to his annual list of recommendations.

I'm not knocking non-fiction. Emmanuel Carrère's *The Adversary* (2000) and Truman Capote's *In Cold Blood* (1966) are as gripping as any novel. Non-fiction authors have educated me in amazing ways. Step forward Miranda Carter (*Anthony Blunt: His Lives*, 2002), Matthew Walker (*Why We Sleep*, 2017), Davis Miller (*The Tao of Bruce Lee*, 2000) and many, many others. What these books have in common is an ability to connect with the reader through their use of insightful examples and high-empathy tales. Or, if you prefer a simple word, 'stories'.

Self-help books rely on certainty, while fiction thrives on ambiguity. If you're writing a self-help book on, say, confidence in the workplace, you need your examples to be relevant to as many readers as possible. This obliges authors to replace complexity with simplicity, which is definitely not a bad thing. But it does tend to produce a binary view of the world – 'assertiveness is always good, meekness is always bad.' A novel is more adept at showing the grey areas of life. Each revelation changes what we think about the hero, the villain and the story. Instead of living by 'always' or 'never', we are open to 'perhaps' and 'maybe'.

The FAB response desired by many self-help books is predominantly action: 'Do this to feel happier', 'Don't eat that if you want more energy.' Changing thoughts and beliefs is important, but only as the means to encourage a change in actions. Fiction encourages us to change our feelings and beliefs by showing extraordinary characters in challenging situations. It forces us to think how we would react if we saw the dripping dagger in front of us.

It's not my intention to come across as scathing about non-fiction books. I read a lot of them, but in this chapter I want to focus on the benefits of fiction.

# Why reading makes you a better person

**I've seen a million slides on creativity at work, but nothing has made as much impact as this story:**

> *A grandfather tells his young grandson that in every person there are two wolves, who live in one's breast and who are always at war with each other. The first wolf is very aggressive and full of violence and hate toward the world. The second wolf is peaceful and full of light and love. The little boy anxiously asks his grandfather which wolf wins. The grandfather replies, 'The one you feed.'[1]*

One thing I love about this quotation by Maryanne Wolf (a polymath experienced in cognitive neuroscience, English literature, linguistics and dyslexia) is that it creates new meaning from an old story.

→ **We learn in-demand twenty-first-century skills from novels.** Creativity is about more than being able to change the colours in an Excel chart. Emotional intelligence depends on a willingness to see the world from another person's point of view. Communication skills – and I'm prioritizing listening over talking here – are boosted when we commit to understanding.

You can take loads of courses and read loads of non-fiction books to learn these vital skills. Or you can read novels.

→ **Fiction lets us enter the mind of someone else.** Closed-mindedness is all around us. You'll never see a flare-up on Twitter or Facebook end with the phrase 'I've read and considered your posts and now I'm changing my mind.' Even

---

1    A Native American story quoted in Maryanne Wolf, *Reader, Come Home: The Reading Brain in a Digital World* (2018).

The only band that matters – The Clash.

innocuous discussions about music, such as who was the best ever punk band in the world, end up with entrenched opinions and unnecessary insults. (It was The Clash, of course, sucker.)

Novels encourage us to feel emotions that are beyond our normal lives, such as the doubts that afflict a superhero and the regrets that haunt a thief thirty years after her last crime. Novels encourage us to experience events that are beyond our imagination; who can resist being intrigued by the opening of Alice Sebold's *The Lovely Bones* (2002), which begins *after* the main character has died?

> My name was Salmon, like the fish; first name,
> Susie. I was fourteen when I was murdered on
> December 6, 1973.

### → <u>Novels open our minds to places we've never been and times we can never visit.</u>

If I want to feel what life was like in nineteenth-century Paris, Victor Hugo's *Les Misérables* (1862) is my best route to the past. Reading makes a deeper impact than a film ever can,

*Dr No*, the first Bond movie, was released in 1962.
No other film franchise has sixty years of audience loyalty.

which is one of the reasons we always say 'The film's not as good as the book' when we leave the cinema.

### → Fiction shows us the complexity of people's motivations.

Not every hero is as morally certain as James Bond; not every villain is as evil as Ernst Stavro Blofeld, Francisco Scaramanga or Dr No. Literature demonstrates that villains have motives that they believe are virtuous and justified. When we first meet Macbeth, he is a fearless warrior who has saved his country; even at the height of his murderous fury he is troubled by his conscience. By showing both the positive and negative implications of ambition, Shakespeare shows us the humanity in every monster.

### → Novels show us how we co-exist.

*A Brief History of Seven Killings* (2014) by Marlon James, the first Jamaican novelist to win the Booker Prize, is a magnificent crime story spanning continents and decades.

We listen to twelve different narrators and meet more than seventy different characters. But James's writing is so skilful that we never lose sight of how the drug lords, slum kids, gunmen and covert FBI operatives are connected through crime, idealism, identity and politics.

## → Emotionally involving books stop us from making snap judgements.

Humans are always looking for shortcuts. We're hardwired to see someone as either part of our tribe or a threat to our survival. For thousands of years these shortcuts helped our ancestors get safely back to their caves after a gruelling day of hunting and gathering.

The psychological concept of cognitive closure means we rarely change our minds about people.[2] And then confirmation bias kicks in, so that everything a person says or does reinforces our original opinion. By contrast, novels and plays encourage us to modify our first impressions. By showing us the complexity of a character, they show us the complexity of everyone we meet.

## → Literature helps you understand people.

No convincing villain in literature has ever done evil just because they're bad.[3] You don't need to like them or accept their justifications, but listening to their inner monologue may help you understand your boss's frustration or the secret pain suffered by that quiet guy, John, who didn't even come to the leaving drinks you organized for him way back in Chapter 2.

You can learn a lot from novels with unreliable narrators. This might be deliberate, as in *The Murder of Roger Ackroyd* (1926) by Agatha Christie, where the village doctor who tells the story has his own secrets. Or it may be down to a lack of knowledge (the second Mrs de Winter in Daphne du Maurier's

---

2      Cognitive closure describes our drive to eliminate ambiguity from our lives. It's often achieved by coming to definite conclusions without sufficient evidence. We can all be irrational in this search for rational certainty.

3      OK, Iago in *Othello*. Maybe.

masterful *Rebecca*, 1938) or shocking parental lies (the confused 10-year-old hero of *The Wasp Factory* by Iain Banks, 1984). Taking these narrators at face value is a dangerous mistake.

# I want you to read more. And you want you to read more as well

**I spend more time reading than on any other activity except sleeping. But I know that some of you may need some help to get the bookish habit back or even start it for the first time.**

The charity I set up, the Margate Bookie, offers bibliotherapists, kind-hearted souls who provide you with a tailored list of recommended books. Obviously, I can't do this for the countless millions reading *The Story Is Everything*, but I can provide you with a bridge between your working life and literature.

How about reading some novels about work? This is a deliberately eclectic list; I want to show you that I practise what I preach and read outside my comfort zone.

*Studs Terkel's Working: A Graphic Adaptation* **(2009) by Harvey Pekar and Paul Buhle** The original book of interviews is great, but this graphic novel moves these tough stories of blue-collar life into another dimension.

*The Mayor of Casterbridge* **(1886) by Thomas Hardy** The rivalry between the traditional Michael Henchard and the innovative Donald Farfrae over farming technology sets up years of conflict. This is much more than a Victorian version of VHS v. Betamax; it's a clash between the old ways and the new.

*The Devil Wears Prada* **(2003) by Lauren Weisberger** You say chick lit, I say a fascinating study of the psychology of office life. All the classics of behavioural science are here: de-individualization, obedience, conformity, even the Milgram Experiment. Plus, great shoes. Admittedly a surprising choice, but it does remind me of my time as a top international catwalk model.[4]

4     Not really.

*The Bees* (2014) **by Laline Paull** A gripping novel about Flora 717, a lowly sanitation bee fighting for survival in a hive riven with secrets and back-stabbing. If you ever wondered why hierarchical organizations exist, this book will be a revelation.

*The Feast of the Goat* (2001) **by Mario Vargas Llosa** Set in the Dominican Republic during the reign of the dictator Rafael Trujillo, this is a terrifying novel about corruption, machismo, power politics and the limits of loyalty. It's by no means focused on work, but the description of the ailing – yet still brutal – Trujillo is the best portrayal of a despotic boss I've ever read.

# Genius reads

**I always pay attention when someone recommends a book to me. I want to know why they choose it, what impact it has had on their life, what made it stand out from the thousands of other books out there. I love it when a book tip opens my mind to a new experience or a different way of interpreting the world.**

I feel an obligation when people ask me for recommendations of books to improve their writing skills. I don't want to waste their precious time, so I always have a selection prepared. I'm going to use our old friends ethos, pathos and logos to convince you of my choices (see chart opposite).

You'll notice that these books are about storytelling, rather than about business. That's deliberate. Start with the story, and the business will follow.

# Tips to enjoy your reading more

**Lockdown has weakened our ability to concentrate. We've doom-scrolled and zapped around YouTube, but nothing seems to stick. I want to suggest some ways you can find solace in a good book.**

→ **Plan your reading time.** I'm never without a book, so I can always squeeze in a few pages while waiting at the dentist.

| | ETHOS | PATHOS | LOGOS |
|---|---|---|---|
| Stephen King *On Writing: A Memoir of the Craft* (1999) | He's got exactly the right arc for this subject. From penniless early days of struggle to publishing over 60 novels, he's done it all. | Midway through writing this book, King was hit by a van and suffered such serious injuries that he feared he'd never write again. His physical and psychological recovery is a big part of the book. | The man's sold 350 million books. He's clearly doing something right. Film adaptations of his work include *The Shawshank Redemption*, *The Shining*, *Carrie* and *Stand By Me*. |
| Julia Cameron *The Artist's Way: A Spiritual Path to Higher Creativity* (1992) | From the despair of drug and alcohol dependency to a life brimming with artistic endeavour, she's lived it. | This is a book about how unlocking your creativity can lead to spiritual growth. The writing tips are important, but ultimately this is a very superior self-help book. | One of Cameron's key tenets is the idea of Morning Pages. This is the daily practice of stream-of-consciousness writing that you do just after waking up. It's a discipline that works for many. |
| Haruki Murakami *What I Talk about When I Talk about Running* (2007) | Who better to tell you about the links between writing and exercise than a novelist who runs ultra-marathons? | Pain's a big part of this autobiography. Murakami doesn't flinch from the gruesome details of struggle and frustration, so you cheer his every success. | Writing is putting one word after another, running is putting one foot after another. You've got to start and then you've got to stick with it. |

But I also schedule half an hour a day for uninterrupted reading. I love the feeling of switching everything off and escaping.

→ **Be realistic.** This is especially important if you've not been a big reader before. Reading isn't a competitive discipline, so don't be swayed by people who claim they can speed-read *War and Peace* in two days or have read 500 books this year.

→ **Plan your next read.** If you enjoyed the Ian Rankin book you've just finished, you're certain to enjoy its companions in the Inspector Rebus series. But your current book can also suggest your next read in more subtle ways. Perhaps the location of a novel is so intriguing that you follow up with a book on local architecture or even a travel guide.

→ **Not all books are right for you.** Should you persevere with a book you don't like? No. There are millions of other options, so take them.

## Where to Next?

To follow up these themes, look at:

Chapter 4: In Part 1, I talked a lot about what people want from a story. What books are Useful, Interesting or Enjoyable for you?

Chapter 11: Remember the adjectives you hope describe your voice. Read three novels, then revise the list.

→ **Do this.** Always have a great book to recommend. If you're part of the select band who have got to this page, you'll want to share your ideas with like-minded geniuses. Tell your listener what impact the book had on you, and why you think they should read it.

# CHAPTER 18

# Turning dull data into exciting stories

Statistics and analysis promote new ideas, change our strategies and help us make vital decisions. It's a crying shame that so many corporate communications are wrecked by the chronic misuse of numbers.

# Nobody likes numbers in presentations

**Many of us would prefer an eternity in Purgatory to yet another yawnfest of graphs sloppily copied from Excel into PowerPoint.**

This law even applies to people who studied maths at university and qualified as accountants, and whose favourite hobby is counting things. Which is a shame, because there's a real value in numbers.

The Covid-19 crisis provides us with many sobering examples of the poor presentation of statistics. In many countries, government explanations of the R-rate and social distancing were so vague and confusing that people ignored them or even did the exact opposite of what was desired. Even with their lives at risk, the audience wasn't engaged.

→ **Technology is our enemy in two very different ways.**

Data is all around us, spewed out by computers without end. We 'drown in data' and suffer from 'data-dumping'. There's too much of it.

At the same time Microsoft Office gives us false hope. We can all turn a column of numbers into a colourful pie chart, and some of us can even make it 3D. But the tool doesn't turn us into a designer, no more than a new dictionary turns us into Charles Dickens. We need to work harder to get our message across.

Your presentation won't win an Oscar and your PowerPoints will never be nominated for an Emmy. The techniques I'm going to teach you in this section won't get you a Hollywood agent or lunch at the Ivy, but they will make your audience sit up. You're not aiming for the red carpet, but you are hoping for an audience that is still awake when the lights are turned back on.

I'm going to use the Margate Bookie as our example. I'll show you some of the mistakes I made so you don't repeat them.

# Changing your mindset about presentations

**The dislike of graphs hits your audience at a hormonal level. They stop listening after twenty seconds, and their eyes glaze over at forty. After a minute they can't remember the day of the week, let alone the title of your presentation.**

You'll often hear the phrase **raw data**, which I think of as **raw ingredients**. The market for stale bread dipped in water, cod eggs and lemon juice is tiny until they're whipped up with a little olive oil into taramasalata. The hungry people sitting in front of me aren't interested in my shopping list. They want to enjoy the finished dish.

There are four steps to follow when you need to change raw data into information that changes your audience's feelings, actions or beliefs.

→ **Step 1: Collect your data.**

At the Margate Bookie we use short feedback forms to learn about our audience. They're the best way we have to capture objective data about our visitors.

**Speedy Feedback**

What session did you attend?

MARK BILLINGHAM/CRIME FICTION

Where do you live?

MARGATE

Have you ever visited Turner Contemporary before?

NO!

→ **Step 2: Turn your data into information.**

A stack of 500 responses has no value unless we turn it into information. Raw data needs to become words.

What did I learn from the feedback forms? That 29 per cent of visitors who live within 5km had never visited Turner Contemporary before. That's incredibly valuable information for us because we can show that the festival appeals to local people and brings them into cultural venues for the first time.

→ **Step 3: Transmit your data.**

Your stand-up presentation has to be very different from your written document. Don't fall into the trap of just talking through your numbers. That's not what your audience wants.

Documents don't transmit. Transmission works only when you realize that the same approach will not succeed for both the document and the presentation. You have to make them different. Facts and figures are best studied on a screen or printout; making an impact on a live audience demands different skills.

A document is a fixed entity. You can present a very high level of detail, even to the extent of including appendices in your slide pack.[1] But you have a low level of control over its reception. You don't know if your intended audience assiduously studies every graph or deletes your email without even opening it.

A presentation is diametrically different. You have limited time before people get bored, so you should include numbers only if they are vital. But your level of control is much higher. You can adapt to the audience by selecting the focus, changing speed or modifying your voice.

→ **Step 4: Transmit knowledge to your audience.**

How do you know you've succeeded in a presentation? When your data becomes the audience's knowledge. You'll know this has happened when you get questions on what people can do with this knowledge, and how it affects *their* audience. What was once a pile of feedback forms is now freshly minted knowledge.

---

1    *Appendix* is Latin for 'This will never be read but hopefully people will think I've done a lot of work.'

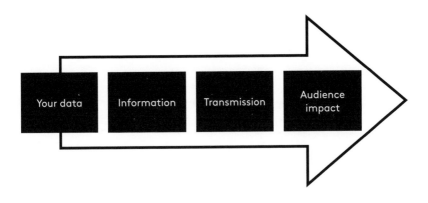

## Better ways to transmit your data and information

**Most graphs are cluttered and hard to read. Often, they're skipped or misunderstood, which is a pain because we usually have to spend a lot of time producing them.**

Here are three graphing techniques that aren't super-common. They'll make you stand out as a good presenter without forcing you to pull an all-nighter.

→ **The infographic**

At the Margate Bookie, we first used a pie chart (see overleaf) to show where our visitors came from. But the biggest number – the 71 per cent who had already visited the venue – took visual precedence. Instead, we wanted our readers to focus on the 29 per cent who *hadn't* visited before.

We underestimate the power of a single number. Use an infographic when there's one really big fact that stops people in their tracks or makes your argument conclusively.

The 29 per cent infographic (also overleaf) is much clearer. It's so powerful that we actually highlighted it on the cover of our report. And, instead of fiddling with Excel for 20 minutes, it took me 45 seconds.

What's our big learning here? Just because you can make a graph in Excel doesn't mean you have to.

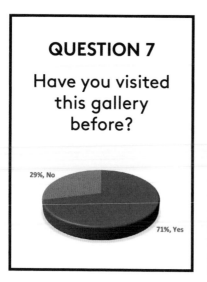

**QUESTION 7**

Have you visited this gallery before?

29%, No

71%, Yes

**29%**

of our visitors had never visited the gallery before

### → <u>The heat map</u>

We needed a table to show what events were selling most tickets a month before the date of the festival. This helped the marketing department focus its resources on less popular sessions. The message had to be detailed (with exact percentages of tickets sold) while also being easy to interpret.

Tables are OK if we have them in front of us. A printed copy means you can run your finger down a column or across a row to find the result you need. Using them live, however, is a fatal mistake. Our marketing team had to concentrate on a table on the screen behind me – which meant they couldn't listen to me.

A heat map highlights the most relevant numbers. The eye is attracted to the darker boxes, which is where we're suffering from low sales. I also turned the font white for any number at 25 per cent or below. Getting rid of the thick box lines and the shading for venues and genres means the team focuses on data rather than design.

You can produce a heat map in Excel using Conditional Formatting.

|  | | Turner Contemporary | Sands Hotel |
|---|---|---|---|
| **BEFORE** | Crime | 80% | 85% |
| | Non-fiction | 72% | 25% |
| | Gala night | 47% | 43% |
| | Debut authors | 14% | 67% |

|  | | Turner Contemporary | Sands Hotel |
|---|---|---|---|
| **AFTER** | Crime | 80% | 85% |
| | Non-fiction | 72% | 25% |
| | Gala night | 47% | 43% |
| | Debut authors | 14% | 67% |

## → The slope graph

Volunteers are a huge part of the Margate Bookie's success. They shift chairs, sell tickets, calm authors' nerves and collect feedback. I'm always interested in why they give us their valuable time, so we commissioned a survey on their motivation. I also wanted to learn if their motivation changed over time, so we compared the results in 2017 to those in 2020.

We ran a focus group and collected our volunteers' three most important reasons for being involved. As a two-line bar chart (see overleaf) it's OK, but readers had to put in effort to find the meaning.

Instead, we used a slope graph (also overleaf) with these three categories. It's easy to see which motivations became more important between 2017 and 2020, and by how much.

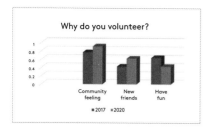

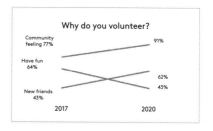

My final point is one you should always bear in mind. No amount of snazziness or technical wizardry will make an irrelevant graph popular with your audience.

# How best to use the storytelling techniques you already know

**Stories hold the key to communicating data. They release a trio of happy chemicals – serotonin, oxytocin, dopamine – that keep the limbic system buzzing. This part of the brain loves feelings and emotions. A list of sales per warehouse just can't compete with the power of stories.**

In Chapter 8 we talked about the left and right brains. Most data is mined by analysts with a heavy quant background, who are normally left-brain dominant. The column of numbers is more important than the aesthetics of their final presentation. The methodical left brain is separated from the more creative right brain by a groove called the longitudinal fissure. Data must leap across from the left to the right brain of the audience, like a reluctant commando storming over a wall into a field full of landmines.

Weird simile, no? I've used it deliberately to mimic that millisecond of cognitive load we feel when we switch between cerebral hemispheres. And it's in this millisecond that your audience senses frustration and confusion and may even start to dislike you.

So, let's remind ourselves of three storytelling mindsets before we proceed.

### → <u>Believe in your spirit as a storyteller.</u>

None of this will amount to a hill of beans unless you believe in your role. You are a storyteller now, not a recently hired data analyst or the wizened head of technology. You must believe in the audience's need for the subject, be it motivations for a merger, how the pandemic has changed all your budget plans, or which entertainment platforms gross the most during lockdowns.

### → <u>Kill your darlings.</u>

Drip your data into the presentation only when it's needed. Use information like the brief guest appearance of a favourite character actor, rather than the main star. Kurt Vonnegut probably wasn't thinking of your presentation when he wrote 'have the guts to cut', but it's very smart advice.

If your numbers are timely and relevant, you'll experience that magic melding of story and information. You'll be showing, rather than telling, and that's why your audience will love you.

### → <u>Think about your audience.</u>

What's in it for them? You've got to show them Useful, Interesting or Enjoyable from the very beginning. If you want to influence them, you have to focus on what they want to change.

I'm very rigorous about this. I'm simply not prepared to waste my time turning hard-won data into attention-grabbing stories, only to realize that I'm speaking to the wrong people. So, I talk to clients about what they want before I pen a single word. I want to save my time as much as I want to save theirs.

## You can turn data into a person

**This is my top tip, but it's also the hardest thing to do. Can you find an example that illustrates the number *and simultaneously* creates an emotional response? You're turning data into a character.**

Let me return to Margate Bookie's 29 per cent stat. We ran a poetry and photography course for local people between the ages of 16 and 24. Many of them were long-term unemployed and several suffered from a mental illness. The quality of work was really high, so we decided to display it on a wall in the gallery.

During the festival, a lady appeared in the bookshop and asked to see the poems up on the walls of the Turner. She seemed a bit intimidated by the crowds, but she told me, with a tear in her eye, that her grandson's pictures were on the wall ...

That little flicker of emotion you feel – joy for the granny, her pride in her grandson – is what happens when your raw data becomes human. What was once a percentage is now a person.

## Where to Next?

To follow up these themes, look at:

- Chapter 4: Remind yourself of the triangle of Useful, Interesting and Enjoyable. It's your obligation to give your audience at least one reason to keep listening to you.

- Chapter 5: Good design of transmittable data gets through the barriers to communication.

→ Do this. Next time you watch a presentation or read a document, identify where a well-chosen number or hard-hitting fact would improve the experience. It's very easy to be negative and point out problems. It takes much more creativity to use information with impact.

# CHAPTER 19

# Grab 'em with headlines and loglines

We send our writing out into a world of competing messages, where our readers are bombarded with one communication after another. You must learn the skills of the professionals to stand out from the crowd.

# You need a hook to catch an audience

**And now, after all that hard work on heroes and worthy opponents, three-act structures and emotional rollercoasters, you've crafted a story that's as intricate and durable as a spider's web. It's full of twists and turns, obstacles and emotions, specific details and universal appeal.**

You think it's all over, but there's one final task for you. And it's a tough one. You must boil the essence of the story down into a single sentence.

Whether you call this a sound bite or an elevator pitch, you need something that's both short and detailed for when people ask 'What's your story about?' I'm not talking about a synopsis, which is a summary of your story in one or two pages. Nor am I talking about the praise that makes up the blurb on the back of a book. I'm talking about a single line that sums up your tale while making it come alive in the reader's mind.

This is a big ask. Luckily, we have headline writers and movie publicists to guide us.

# The golden age of the tabloids

**The best-paid workers at newspapers weren't star journalists or big-name editors. It was the headline writers who made the big bucks. I was always in awe of their skill. With just five words on a poster they could entice millions into buying a paper. Their headlines promised intrigue and scandal. They could make you tremble in fear or laugh out loud with a glorious pun.**

Our headlines are online now. They've got to work even harder to grab the attention of distracted eyes and speed-scrolling brains.

Here are five ways you can use their techniques to produce an alluring summary to entice readers.

→ **Personal appeal.** The most shared article on Facebook in 2019 had nothing to do with the Kardashians or Donald Trump. Instead, it was 'Suspected Child Predator May Be in Our Area'.

The fear this headline provokes is tangible. Our emotions are fully engaged, and we have to find out more. As a parent it's impossible *not* to click on the link. With a gasp of relief we realize that 'our area' is thousands of miles away.

The words 'you', 'your', 'us' and 'our' are always a good way to make readers feel an article is for them. They suggest a special bond between reader and writer.

→ **The unexpected question.** I love a headline that makes me ponder. Twitter and Facebook reduce all the colours of the world to black and white, so I appreciate the odd touch of grey. Ambiguity can be attractive in a world of yes and no. I very rarely read *The Spectator*, but I had to click on the article 'Is Donating to Large Charities a Waste of Time?' because it was an idea that I'd never thought about before.

→ **The numbered list.** We fall for '10 Things You Didn't Know about Lizzo/*Better Call Saul*/West Ham United' every time.

Why? We're certain the article will be short, which is a good thing in this time-pressured world. It promises us a quick way to get up to date on a topic we know nothing about. We don't want to become a Subject Matter Expert on the singer/series/football club, but we do want enough knowledge to talk about them.

Headlines with numbers – '7 Facts', '3 Reasons' – hint at an appealing mix of maximum knowledge and minimum effort. We expect to gain from reading the article.

→ **Learning and change.** Have you ever wondered why so many headlines include the phrase 'will make you'?

The phrase[1] implies a causal link between the content of the article (yoga, say, or a new diet) and its impact on the reader (breathe easier, feel lighter, be happier). It's a compelling proposition. Your world will magically improve because 'Reading books will make you rich' and 'Travelling the world will make you wise.'

You can appeal to the human desire for self-improvement with words such as 'tips', 'hacks', 'secrets' and 'insights'. Use 'lessons I learned' for a more personal touch.

---

1    Variations include 'will get you' and 'will turn you into'.

*Amélie*

Let me put these ideas into action. The introduction to this section is the deliberately wordy 'Here are five ways you can use their techniques to produce an alluring summary to entice readers.' It's OK, but not good enough for a chapter on writing headlines. Try this instead: 'What five secrets will make your audiences love your headlines?'[2]

## Learn from the masters of Hollywood

**Loglines distil the essential elements of a movie into one sentence. They're used by movie-biz insiders to sum up a film in a single sentence.**

Great loglines are tiny masterpieces of the writing craft, and we can learn a lot about speedy, effective communication by looking at examples.

Loglines are different from taglines, which are designed to

---

2    I've reduced this section intro to a ten-word headline. It's an unexpected question that contains a personal appeal to the emotions (*love*). I've used 'your' twice, promised a numbered list and used the intriguing word 'secrets'. The phrase 'will make you' suggests that it's of immediate use to the reader.

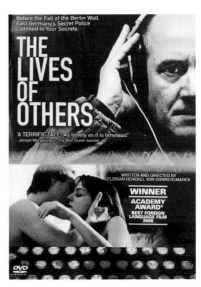

The Social Network                                    The Lives of Others

go on posters to market the movie to the public. My favourite
taglines include:

*Amélie* 'One person can change your life forever'

*The Social Network* 'You don't get to 500 million friends
without making a few enemies'

*The Lives of Others* 'Before the fall of the Berlin Wall, East
Germany's secret police listened to your secrets'

Good taglines pique our curiosity. We want to meet the
mysterious Amélie and the man with half a billion friends.
The half-hidden rhyme (fall, Wall) and the repeated 'secrets'
intrigue us. We queue for tickets to solve these mysteries.

Loglines are different. They're used by film-industry
professionals to boil down a movie's essential narrative. The
tagline for *Alien* – 'In space no one can hear you scream' –
looks great on a poster but doesn't say enough to a producer,
actor or financier. The logline is what they need: 'The crew
of a space vessel fight for their survival when an apparently
indestructible creature invades their ship.'

Loglines follow set patterns. I'm going to show you one
that combines four elements.

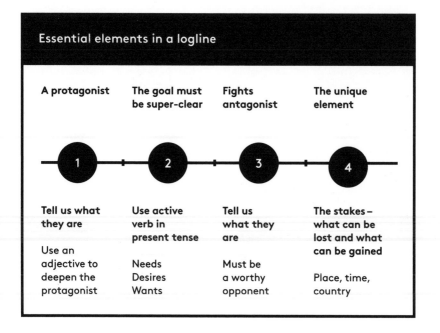

Essential elements in a logline

| A protagonist | The goal must be super-clear | Fights antagonist | The unique element |
|---|---|---|---|
| **1** | **2** | **3** | **4** |
| Tell us what they are | Use active verb in present tense | Tell us what they are | The stakes – what can be lost and what can be gained |
| Use an adjective to deepen the protagonist | Needs Desires Wants | Must be a worthy opponent | Place, time, country |

→ **1. Begin with the hero.** Tell the audience what the protagonist is or does: a scientist, a house husband. Use a single adjective to 'deepen' them: unhappy, ambitious, frustrated. There's no need to name them unless they're already known to the audience (Rocky Balboa, Princess Diana).

→ **2. Add a single, absolutely clear goal for the hero.** Use an active verb in the present tense: wants, searches for, yearns for, needs.

→ **3. Introduce the antagonist in the same way as we described the hero:** What they do and a deepening adjective. We need them to be a worthy opponent, which is why we use frightening descriptions: evil genius, twisted firestarter, master criminal, office frenemy.

→ **4. Choose a unique fourth element.** I like to know the stakes. What will the hero gain if she's successful or lose if she fails? Other viewers want to see communities that are different from their own (the Amish in *Witness*, the pagans in *The Wicker Man*), or to visit a time and a place that's new (1950s Los Angeles in

*Chinatown*, futuristic Los Angeles in *Blade Runner*). It's also great if you can suggest an emotional connection.

Here's a logline for *Inception* (2010). It reduces a very complex 148-minute movie to a single sentence. Bear in mind that you've got a very small number of words to make an impact, so it must be mega-reduced. It's logline, not longline, as the wisecrackers in Hollywood would no doubt say:

*A thief who steals corporate secrets through dream-sharing technology is given the inverse task of planting an idea into the mind of a CEO.*

## A quick game for you

**Here are seven movie loglines. What films do they describe? The answers are hidden away on page 189 to stop you cheating.**

→ 1. A depressed suburban father in a midlife crisis decides to turn his hectic life around after becoming infatuated with his daughter's attractive friend.

→ 2. A Phoenix secretary embezzles forty thousand dollars from her employer's client, goes on the run, and checks in to a remote motel run by a young man under the domination of his mother.

→ 3. A group of seven former college friends gathers for a weekend reunion at a South Carolina winter house after the funeral of one of their friends.

→ 4. A young woman is hired as a maid to a Japanese heiress, but she is secretly involved in a plot to steal her money.

→ 5. A boy who communicates with spirits seeks the help of a disheartened child psychologist.

→ 6. The eldest son in a family of unemployed adults skilfully leads an invasion into the home of a wealthy family.

→ 7. A frightened young girl must find her missing parents in a secret world full of witches, monsters, gods and talking animals.

# Now it's your turn to create some loglines

**Stick to the four-element approach to tell people about the last film you enjoyed or a novel you loved. If you're feeling bold you can also come up with a logline for the next story you're going to tell.**

| Prompt | |
|---|---|
| Protagonist (remember the adjective) | |
| Goal | |
| Antagonist | |
| Unique element | |

Producing punchy one-liners is hard work. It's far easier to write flabby sentences, but those aren't what the audience wants. You need to cut out all unnecessary detail to get to the heart of the tale.

Don't be too concerned by the differences between headlines and loglines. Use whatever technique works for you. You want an audience for your story, so take whatever you need.

As my final proof, look at these two messages about Walt Disney. If you prefer the first one, you might have to read this book again!

*The Walt Disney Company's objective is to be one of the world's leading producers and providers of entertainment and information, using its portfolio of brands to differentiate its content, services and consumer products. The company's primary goals are to maximize earnings and cash flow, and to allocate capital toward growth initiatives that will drive long-term shareholder value.*

Walt Disney Mission Statement 2013

*If you can dream it, you can do it.*

Walt Disney

## Where to Next?

To follow up these themes, look at:

- Chapter 7: A logline is a hero's journey in its shortest form.

- Chapter 10: Can you improve the short summaries (you can call them 'loglines' now) that I wrote for each tale?

- Chapter 11: Headlines should also reflect the voice of the stories that follow them.

→ <u>Be alive</u> to the next ten headlines you see. If you skip the story, work out why it didn't grab your attention. If you read on, ask yourself what buttons the headline pushed.

# CHAPTER 20

# Where to now?

And now the end is near, so let's face the future with some suggestions of what to think about next ...

## 'Talent borrows, but genius steals'

**Over the years I've seen this quotation ascribed to T.S. Eliot, Oscar Wilde, Steve Jobs, Pablo Picasso and even Morrissey. It's a wonder Aristotle doesn't have a claim on it. But take care: just because a quotation is everywhere doesn't mean it's true.**

There's a lot of meaning to unpack from these five words. It can be read as an encouragement to create at any cost – 'even the greats have copied ideas'. Some interpret it as a plagiarist's apology – 'everyone steals from someone else' – while others see it as an exhortation to be honest about our artistic influences.

Unfortunately, it also sets up a distinction between people who are OK at writing (the merely 'talented') and those who operate at a higher level than mere mortals (the 'geniuses'). And the word 'genius' suggests that some people are just born to be better at writing than others.

In our last chapter together I'm going to play around with these ideas. My aim is to give you as many tips as I can about your new life as a storyteller, writer and presenter.

## Seven rapid-fire ideas to support you

→ **We are all born with the story instinct.** Your audience want to hear stories. They'll all want you to succeed, and they'll forgive you if you take a risk.

→ **Write every day.** You've got writing muscles and they need to be limber and strong. It really doesn't matter if you do it brilliantly or badly, for seconds or for hours, but you have to keep practising.

→ **Write on stolen paper.** My only vice is that I was once an assiduous and gifted 'borrower' of office supplies. First drafts are normally rubbish, so be prepared to throw them away without a second thought. Keep those lovely Moleskine notebooks for your love poetry and the final versions of your haikus.

→ **Useful, Interesting and Enjoyable.** As ever, it's about the reader's needs. Make it clear that your blogpost is of immediate benefit or will help them in the future.

→ **Good writers are always great readers.** Find writers whose work you like and work out why you like it. This isn't a license to steal, but an encouragement to look for structures that work and to listen to more voices.

→ **Rereading a favourite book is always an amazing experience.** Go back to the articles and books that have changed your FAB, analysing what they did to affect you so deeply. Once you understand why *Dracula* leaves you cold but *The Strange Case of Dr Jekyll and Mr Hyde* keeps you up all night, you'll become a better storyteller.

→ **Feedback is vital in your development.** Find someone whose work is of a high standard and ask for help. Do your best to distinguish between short-term help ('change the font before you send it out') and advice that will improve your writing dramatically in the long term ('use pathos to create a loyal readership').

Why seven ideas? It seems to be a magic number for storytelling – think Brides, Brothers, Psychopaths, Dwarves, Sins, Pillars of Wisdom, Habits of Successful People, Sisters, Daughters of Eve and Years in Tibet. And if you're looking for a movie where structure is everything, take a look at the outstanding *Se7en* (1995), but don't blame me if you have nightmares.

# Your mindset is as important as your skill

**You know the nuts and bolts of narrative technique and you know what your audience wants from you.**

But is there a sneering voice between your ears that wants to knock your confidence? Or does a bad memory – the professor who failed your essay, the job application where you mis-spelled your own name – flare up in your mind?

Check in with how you feel. I still get a bit nervous before I start a story, and I often want to give up halfway through.

Negative emotions are there for a reason, and it's dangerous to ignore the tension in our stomach or the occasional fluttering of our cheeks. But don't let any of that stop you writing.

Here's what you need to tell yourself at this time:

→ **We are all naturally good at storytelling.** Creativity is a gift we all have, so please feel free to reject any limiting assumptions you have about your ability – and your right – to tell stories.

→ **Writers are made, not born.** None of us was born with a pen in our hands. Skills must be learned and practised. The best writers are those who have worked many long, hard hours to develop their natural storytelling ability into something magical. Let go of the myth of the solitary genius who was born to write thousand-page novels.

→ **Perfection doesn't exist, but sadly perfectionism does.** Writing is about banging out the words, revising them with the help of others, and getting them out into the world. I'm not giving you permission to be sloppy or slapdash, obviously. But there always comes a time when you have to accept that your story is ready to be told.

## Where to Next?

To follow up these themes, look at:

- Chapter 21: Books are constrained by factors such as size and number of pages. (Normally this is positive, because it encourages a tight focus on themes.) What would you like to see covered next?

→ <u>Read this.</u> I don't want you to read any more books about storytelling or business writing. But I do want you to read novels and creative non-fiction. Which would you recommend to a friend?

<u>**Do you remember what I said about not liking long introductions?**</u> I'm the same about long goodbyes. I hope you've learned as much from reading *The Story Is Everything* as I did from writing it. And I hope you've enjoyed the journey as much as I did.

Who knows when we will meet again? I'm up for a sequel if you are ...

→ **Answers to pages 181**

1. *American Beauty*
2. *Psycho* – but is the secretary really the protagonist? I believe most viewers have forgotten her by the time they've met Norman and his mum
3. *The Big Chill*
4. *The Handmaiden*
5. *The Sixth Sense* – but again, I wonder if the real protagonist is the Bruce Willis character
6. *Parasite*
7. *Spirited Away*

# Picture credits

# Index

**A**

adverbs 41

adverts 19–21, 32
  Spanish Christmas lottery
    (el Gordo) 26–8

Aristotle 147–8

audience 35–6
  adapt to the audience 108,
    110, 173
  emotional connection to
    audience 149–51
  every person in your
    audience is their own
    hero 72
  knowing how and when to
    use your facts 152–4
  personal credibility 148–9
  taking the audience on a
    journey 67–70
  top tips to keep your
    audience with you 37–8

authorities 23, 24–5, 153

**B**

Boorman, Arthur 82–4

brain function 74
  left and right hemispheres
    74–6

**C**

Campbell, Joseph *The Hero
  with a Thousand Faces* 67

Cialdini, Robert *Influence: T
  he Psychology of Persuasion*
  23–6

communication barriers 47
  hospital settings 47–50
  how to get through the
    barriers 52–3
  Richness and Spread 50–1

conflict 83–4
  conflicts are vital, but
    dilemmas are better 92–3

consistency and commitment
  23, 25

creation myths 84–6
  corporation creation myths
    86–7

creativity, encouraging 76
  become a child again 77

copy without producing
  fakes 77–8
  don't work late 78
  find more time to do
    nothing 78–9
  pretend to be someone
    different 77

**D**

data presentation 166
  better ways to transmit your
    data and information
    169–72
  changing your mindset
    about presentations 167–9
  using storytelling techniques
    172–3
  you can turn data into a
    person 173–4

Dramatic Gap 68–9

**E**

ethos 147, 148–9

**F**

FAB (feelings, actions, beliefs)
  14–15, 27, 52, 68, 79
  adapting your voice to your
    objective 108, 116
  appealing to the emotions
    and to rational thinking
    15–17
  connecting to the client's
    FAB 88–9
  FAB in finance 19–21
  how influencers create
    stories in our minds 17–19
  mission statements 44
  reading 156–7, 186

favours, returning 23, 25–6

feedback 106–7, 117, 137, 186
  advisory feedback 138
  complimentary feedback
    137
  destructive feedback 138
  emotional reactions to
    feedback 139–41
  giving feedback 138–9
  suggestive feedback 137–8

fiction 157–61

Field, Syd *Screenplay: The
  Foundations of Screenwriting*
  60

Flesch Reading Ease Score 38–9

flow 113
  flow at work 117–18
  how to find your flow 114–15
  motivation 116
  preparation 116–17

**G**

graphs 169
  heat maps 170–1
  infographics 169–70
  slope graphs 171–2

**H**

headlines 176–8

Hero's Journey 67
  every person in your
    audience is their own hero
    72, 96–7
  taking the audience on a
    journey 67–70
  the storyteller is not the
    hero 71–2

Holmes, Elizabeth 16–17, 19, 72

Hughes, Ted 'The Thought-
  Fox' 75

**I**

influencing people 14–21
  micro-stories 28–33
  Spanish Christmas lottery
    (el Gordo) 26–8
  using influence in
    storytelling 24–6
  we are all influenced by
    stories 23

introductions 9–12

**J**

jargon 47–8, 129–30

**L**

liking people like ourselves
  23, 25

literature 157–61

loglines 178–81
  create loglines 182–3
  loglines game 181

logos 147, 152–4

**M**

masters of communication
  11–12

Aristotle 147–8
Hollywood loglines
178–81
tabloid headlines 176–8
mentors 69, 71–2, 118
message 99–100
messages about loss are
effective 100
micro-stories 28–9
in the far future 31–3
in the near future 30–1
in the past 29
in the present 30
mission statements 42–3,
44, 183
motivation 116

N
novels 157–61

O
objectives 108, 116

P
passive voice 41
pathos 147, 149–51
presentations 9
factors which change
your voice when you're
presenting 108–9
structuring your
presentations 63–5
taking the audience on a
journey 67–70
see data presentation
proofing (proofreading) 137,
141–2

R
readability 38–40
bizspeak versus humanspeak
42–3, 129, 130
improving readability 40–2
reading 156, 186
genius reads 162–3
read more 161–2
rise of the billionaire
bibliophile 156–7
tips to enjoy your reading
more 162–4
why reading makes you a
better person 157–61
recording yourself 110

S
senses 94–5
sentence length 38, 40–1, 98
Situation, Complication,
Resolution 57–60
Aesop's Fables 57–8
Chocolat 58
Mildred Pierce 59
Working Girl 58–9
social proof 23, 26
Spanish Christmas lottery (el
Gordo) 26–8
speaking 109–10
Sperry, Roger 74
statistics, making interesting
see data presentation
stories 9, 10, 81–2, 101
Useful, Interesting,
Enjoyable 35–6, 173, 186
stories about your organization
81
Foundation Story 84–7
unique personal perspective
109
What We Do and Why We Do
It 88–90
stories about yourself 81
What You Learned by
Overcoming an Obstacle
82–4
storytelling 11, 92
be you 100–1
conflicts are vital, but
dilemmas are better 92–3
keep it simple 97–100
start quickly 96
take people on an emotional
journey 96–7
taking the audience on a
journey 67–70
the storyteller is not the
hero 71–2
use all the senses 94–5
use the vocabulary of
storytelling 133–5
your mindset is as important
as your skill 186–7
structuring stories 57–60,
109, 152
creation myths 85–7
expanding your structure
into three acts 60–3
structure improves your

presentations 63–5
transformation 60
Syd Field Three-act Paradigm
61–3

T
tabloid headlines 176–8
transformation 60, 90

V
voice 105
considering the writers and
presenters you like 107–8
defining how you want to
come across 105–6
factors which change
your voice when you're
presenting 108–9
feedback 106–7
voice and speaking are not
the same 109–10

W
word choice 38, 42, 109, 129
how to avoid the four
biggest word traps 129–32
Roulette Wheel of bad word
choices 132
use the vocabulary of
storytelling 133–5
writing 121, 185
flow 113–18
joy of the blank page
exercise 126–7
ritual, routine, and
regularity 121–3
seven rapid-fire ideas to
support your writing
185–6
where and when do writers
write? 123–5
working conditions 117,
125–6
Writer's Block 121
your mindset is as important
as your skill 186–7

# Acknowledgements

Huge thanks to Lesley Henderson, publisher extraordinaire, who first suggested an online chat.

Kara Hattersley-Smith at LKP/Quercus has been a supportive and enthusiastic commissioning editor. Rosanna Fairhead and Melissa Mellor are great copy-editors, and Jon Allan is a designer with flair and verve.

One thing I've loved about writing *The Story Is Everything* is asking for help. Three friends from Leeds University – Andy Round, John Tague, Peter Cross – all came up with sharp ideas. Richard Bastin and Sheryl Garratt both shaped the book in unexpected ways. Everyone in Team Bookie provided inspiration.

I wrote this book during lockdown, and I'm immensely grateful to all my friends who kept my spirits up. I adore you all, even if I don't always show it.

Right, who fancies a drink?